TRAGEDY OF THE WAHK-SHUM:
THE DEATH OF ANDREW J. BOLON, YAKIMA INDIAN AGENT, AS TOLD BY *SU-EL-LIL*, EYEWITNESS; ALSO, THE SUICIDE OF GENERAL GEORGE A. CUSTER, AS TOLD BY OWL CHILD, EYEWITNESS

by
Lucullus Virgil McWhorter

Edited, with additional material by
Donald M. Hines

Great Eagle Publishing®

TRAGEDY OF THE WAHK-SHUM:
THE DEATH OF ANDREW J. BOLON,
YAKIMA INDIAN AGENT, AS TOLD BY *SU-EL-LIL*, EYEWITNESS;
ALSO, THE SUICIDE OF GENERAL GEORGE A. CUSTER,
AS TOLD BY OWL CHILD, EYEWITNESS

by
Lucullus Virgil McWhorter

Edited, with additional material by
Donald M. Hines

Published by:

Great Eagle Publishing, Inc.
3020 Issaquah-Pine Lake Rd. SE Suite 481
Issaquah, WA 98027-7255 U.S.A.

Copyright © 1994 by Donald M. Hines
First Printing 1994

PUBLISHER'S CATALOGING IN PUBLICATION
(Prepared by Quality Books Inc.)

McWhorter, Lucullus Virgil, 1860-1994
   Tragedy of the Wahk-shum: The Death of Andrew J. Bolon, Yakima Indian Agent, as Told by *Su-el-lil*, Eyewitness; Also, The Suicide of General George A. Custer by Owl Child, Eyewitness/ by Lucullus Virgil McWhorter; edited, with additional material by Donald M. Hines.
   p. cm.
   ISBN 0-9629539-4-6

   1. Bolon, Andrew J. 2. Yakima Indians—History. 3. Custer, George Armstrong, 1839-1876. 4. Little Big Horn, Battle of the, Mont., 1876. 5. Dakota Indians—History. 6. Cheyenne Indians—History. 7. Indians of North America—History—19th century. I. Hines, Donald M., 1931- II. Owl Child. III. Title. IV. Title: Suicide of Gen. Geo. A. Custer.

                    973.0497
E99.Y2M39 1994   QBI94-2121
Library of Congress Catalog Card Number: 94-079277

CONTENTS

ORDER FORM

Che-pow To-cos (Owl Child), also known as *Shat-Taw-Wee* (Leader in Battle), whose English name was Alec McCoy, as warrior. (Photo by L.V. McWhorter, 1923) Historical Photograph Collections #498k(5), Washington State University, Pullman, WA.

I. FOREWORD

by Donald M. Hines

Resembling a Greek tragedy, during mid-September 1855 Yakima Indian Agent Andrew J. Bolon was murdered near present-day Goldendale, WA. Then, on September 24, 1858, the Yakima warrior *Qualchan* was summarily hanged as guilty of Bolon's murder by Col. George Wright[1]—but *Qualchan* was innocent, had been nowhere near the murder scene. Finally, seven years after *Qualchan's* hanging, now General Wright and his wife took passage in San Francisco on the S. S. *Brother Jonathan* to sail northward. In heavy weather about 16 miles northwest of Crescent City, California, the ship struck a reef and broke up, and with others the Wrights perished.[2]

The historical accounts included in this volume are extraordinary, for they comprise an intersection of history—our "book history" with the Native American's singular history recalled from memory and related aloud before listeners. First, at about age 14, Yakima George (*Su-el-lil*, a Klikitat and a sha-

FOREWORD

man) had been witness to the slaying of Indian Agent Bolon during mid-September 1855.

Fearing reprisals from whites, *Sul-el-lil* kept silent until in 1911 and again in 1915 when his account was brought to the attention of L.V. Mc-Whorter, Yakima Valley pioneer and student of Central Washington and Oregon Indian life and culture. A second narrative, also related to McWhorter about 1911, was an eyewitness account by Owl Child (*Chepos To-cos*) from Central Montana Territory of a U.S. Cavalry group which blundered upon a very large Indian village, were set upon by many hundreds of Indian warriors, and were annihilated within minutes. Especially observed was the shameful, cowardly death of the white commander. Based upon internal details given by Owl Child as well as archaeological evidence, we believe Owl Child witnessed the quick destruction suffered by Gen. George Armstrong Custer and his detachment of 7th Cavalry troops.

Both eyewitness accounts by *Su-el-lil* and by Owl Child are singular in that they present historical events in a unique manner, unlike the dry, dusty chronologies of White or Euramerican histories. First, their accounts comprise "seen events of the past" which were observed, even etched into memory. Second, their accounts were subsequently recalled, related, in a group setting. Third, not written, these eyewitness accounts were <u>told</u> across generations. [We must remember that the Southern Plateau Indian tribes had no written language—all was spoken.]

6

TRAGEDY OF THE *WAHK-SHUM*

Fourth, eyewitness accounts were shaped into a <u>traditional form</u>, were tautly constructed; were objective in nature; were terse, not lengthy; and—maddening only to us—lack details of names, individuals, times, places, etc..

Each narrative has been reproduced exactly, word for word, as first given by each Indian narrator. Background data and photos are provided, if available, for each Native American eyewitness. Also, dates when the narratives were first taken down are given. If *Su-el-lil's* account was republished in 1968 by Ye Galleon Press, Fairfield, WA., Owl Child's account has been essentially ignored by "official" historians.

In preparation and organization of this volume, we have employed the 1937 edition of *Tragedy of the Wahk-shum...* which was privately printed by L.V. McWhorter in Yakima, WA. We have edited out obvious infelicities of spelling, punctuation, capitalization and verb tenses while keeping Guie or McWhorter's sentences and paragraphs intact. We have supplied complete versions of McWhorter's references, but have cast them in a modern form. Following this FOREWORD is "INTRODUCTORY" which was prepared by Dean Guie, Yakima Valley writer-acquaintance of McWhorter. Appearing next is *Su-el-lil's* entire account, in English: THE KILLING OF MAJOR BOLON. Then follows McWhorter's account of that late autumn ride into the teeth of a blizzard: LOCATING THE SCENE OF

FOREWORD

THE BOLON TRAGEDY. We have omitted the traditional narratives found in McWhorter's original—these have been included in our *Ghost Voices: Yakima Indian Myths, Legends, Humor, and Hunting Stories.* Also included is Owl Child's "THE DEATH OF GEN. GEORGE A. CUSTER AND HIS COMMAND, AS TOLD BY OWL CHILD— EYEWITNESS." Following this appears all NOTES. Appearing last is ACKNOWLEDGE-MENTS, plus an Order Form.

"*Ow-hi*," Chief of the Ya-ki-mas and brother to *Te-i-as* and *Kam-ma-ai-a-kan* (Painted by Lt. J. K. Duncan, Fall, 1853). S.I.N.A.A. photo 41-242-A.

"Qual-chin," son of *Owhi*, Chief of the Yakimas (painted by Lt. J. K. Duncan, Fall 1853). S.I.N.A.A. photo MNH 1481F.

II. INTRODUCTORY

At *Wahk-shum* Spring in the Simcoe Mountains[3], beside an ancient Indian trail leading from the Yakima Country to Celilo Falls of the Columbia River, a small granite block marks the place of one of the most savage murders in Northwest frontier history.

There, one rainy September day in 1855, Major Andrew J. Bolon, agent to the tribes of Central and Eastern Washington Territory, was done to death by a party of supposedly friendly Yakimas. The deed precipitated the Yakima war of 1855-56 and was the beginning of general Indian hostilities throughout a great part of Washington and Oregon Territories.

With the exception of the victim, no white persons were present, and the few Indians who participated in the killing or who looked on never talked about it to a member of the white race. Not until *Suel-lil (Sul-lil,* as pronounced by some Indians), better known as Yakima George, aged Klikitat medicine man and last survivor of the ghastly affair, opened his heart years afterward to his friend, Lucullus V. McWhorter, and told the whole grim, thrilling

11

story.

Given in the Indian narrator's own words, this, the only eyewitness account on record, is published here for the first time.[4]

McWhorter heard the story from *Suel-lil* in 1911, as interpreted by John Billie, an Indian, the faithfulness of whose rendition was confirmed four years later when *Su-ellil* repeated the tale through his son-in-law, William Charley, also a Klikitat, who had advised McWhorter of its availability.

To none but the three, *Su-el-lil* declared, had he ever related it. Down the long years he had guarded the secret of his presence on the murder ground lest vengeance be wreaked upon him, however innocent he was of spilling Bolon's blood.

That his simple, gripping narrative is true, McWhorter does not doubt, for *Su-el-lil* had a reputation for veracity and dependability. He was an "old time Indian." And that his is the only written, first-hand-story of the incident should be of particular interest to students of Washington Territorial history. In the light of the Klikitat's recital, other published accounts—all based on hearsay--are incomplete, if not inaccurate.

Besides his oral contribution to the cause of history, *Su-el-lil* performed an additional service. In November, 1915, although feeble and suffering from the dreaded malady, trachoma, he guided McWhorter and Charley to the spot on which Bolon was slain, and thus was revealed the exact location of the wilderness

INTRODUCTORY

tragedy, which otherwise never would have been ascertained.

The trip, made on horseback by the trio from the vicinity of White Swan on the Yakima Indian reservation, developed into one of hardships and peril, of cold, hunger, and extreme fatigue, and desperate groping through a raging snowstorm. From the experience *Su-el-lil* did not recover; he died the following year.

As a result of *Su-el-lil's* sacrifice and McWhorter's research, on October 6, 1918, the Washington State Historical Society [Tacoma] dedicated two memorials--the stone marking where Bolon fell, and, in Cedar Valley, Klickitat County, about eleven miles northwest of Goldendale, a roadside monument chronicling the event and giving the position of the marker.

Among the speakers at the dedicatory ceremonies was General Hazard Stevens, seventy-six-year-old son of General Isaac Ingalls Stevens, Washington's first territorial governor, who, in 1854, appointed Bolon agent to the tribes of the vast region extending from the Cascade Range to the Bitteroot Range in what now is the State of Idaho.

In poor health for several months prior to the occasion of the monument dedication, Hazard Stevens hardly had begun his address when he faltered and collapsed. He died five days later in a Goldendale hotel room.

As a boy of twelve years, Hazard Stevens had known Bolon in Olympia. Bolon then, in 1854, was a member of the first territorial legislature, a representative from Clark County. Both were present at the famous Walla Walla Treaty Council, May 29 to June 11, 1855, when Governor Stevens met with the Nez Perces, Umatillas, Cayuses, Walla Wallas, Yakimas, Palooses, Klikitats, and kindred tribes, and persuaded them to cede more than sixty thousand square miles of their lands to the United States.

Three reservations were set aside by the treaty—one with an area of five thousand miles largely in the present states of Idaho and Oregon, including a strip of Southeastern Washington, for the Nez Perces; another for the Umatillas, Walla Wallas, and Cayuses of eight hundred square miles in Northeastern Oregon; and the third including about one million, two hundred thousand acres in South Central Washington for the Yakimas, Klikitats, and twelve other affiliated tribes and bands and designated as the Yakima Nation. With slight boundary changes, the last is the Yakima reservation of today.

The twenty-nine thousand square miles relinquished by the Yakima Nation embraced the present counties of Chelan, Kittitas, Franklin, Adams and Yakima, and large parts of Douglas and Klickitat counties. In return for this cession, the Yakimas were to be paid $140,000-$200,000 in annuities over a 20-year period, and $60,000 (to be spent for them) for the "making of improvements" on their reservation.

Opposed to the treaty from the outset were the principal Yakima chiefs—*Ka-mi-a-kun*;[5] his youn-

INTRODUCTORY

gest brother, *Skloom*;[6] and his brother-in-law, *Ow-hi*.[7]

Their signatures [marks] appear on the treaty paper; but in the case of *Ka-mi-a-kun* and *Ow-hi*, neither meant to sign or approve the document, according to some of the old Yakimas who witnessed the signing. The latter, in after years, informed McWhorter that *Ka-mi-a-kun* and *Ow-hi* merely "touched a stick while a little mark was made to show friendship only." It is McWhorter's belief that they were persuaded to append their marks under the supposition that they were not signing the treaty itself.

Whatever their intentions, *Ka-mi-a-kun* and *Ow-hi*, along with the other head men, were not reconciled to the terms.

At the conclusion of the Walla Walla Council Governor Stevens left with a small party for Fort Benton, east of the Rockies, to treat with the tribes there.

Two days out of Fort Benton on his return journey, on October 29 he was met by an express from The Dalles, Oregon Territory, and told of the murder of Agent Bolon; and the defeat on Toppenish Creek of Brevet Major Granville O. Haller and his command of one hundred men. Haller had marched from Fort Dalles to punish the Yakimas shortly after intelligence of Bolon's death was received at the Columbia River post.

The unwitting instrument that sent Bolon on his fatal ride was Garry, head chief of the Spokanes.

TRAGEDY OF THE *WAHK-SHUM*

About the middle of September, Bolon, en route with treaty goods to the Spokane country, where he was to join Governor Stevens, met Chief Garry on the trail east of The Dalles. Garry informed him that several white prospectors, traveling from Puget Sound to the recently discovered Colville gold fields, had been killed by Indians in the Yakima Valley.[8]

Prior to the treaty-making, the Yakimas had not molested white persons traversing their territory. But they became perturbed by talk at the council of emigrants flooding westward, and by the insistence that the tribes be settled upon reservations to avoid conflict with the newcomers. And when they realized that the greater part of their country was in process of transfer to the United States, they grew resentful and bitter, and advised miners using the Naches Pass trail and wayfarers in general to keep out. Few of the gold hunters paid any attention.

"Not one perhaps of all these eager travelers," says Snowden, "anticipated any trouble from the Indians; certainly none of those who started earliest did. . . .They. . . assumed that the whole Indian country except the reservation was now open to settlement. They had the best of reasons for this assumption, for, immediately after the Walla Walla Council was concluded, official notice that the ceded lands were now open to settlement, signed by Stevens and Palmer [General Joel Palmer, Superintendent of Indian Affairs for Oregon Territory], was published in the newspapers of both Oregon and Washington."[9]

INTRODUCTORY

A footnote to the above reads: "This notice appeared in the *Puget Sound Courier*, published at Steilacoom, on July 12th, while news of the gold discovery at Colville had appeared, for the first time, in the preceding issue on July 5th."

Legally, of course, the Yakimas' title to the ceded lands was not extinguished, and would not be until Congress ratified the treaty, which was not done until 1859.

Chief Garry's report started Bolon at once to investigate. To show his confidence in the Yakimas, he went alone. On September 20 he rode out of The Dalles and headed north on the Indian trail. He intended to question Chief *Ka-mi-a-kun* and thought to find him at his home on Ahtanum Creek, near the Catholic mission, St. Joseph.

At Topppenish Creek, not far from where Fort Simcoe was established in 1856, he came upon the lodge of *Show-a-wai Ko-ti-a-ken*, also known as *Ice*, younger brother of *Ka-mi-a-kun*. Bolon and Ice were friends. Ice warned him that many of the Yakimas were in ugly temper, and urged him to return immediately to The Dalles if he valued his life. Bolon heeded the advice and put his horse to the back trail. That night he camped in the Simcoe Mountains, and in the drizzly dawn he resumed his flight which, ironically enough, was to throw him within a few hours into the very arms of his mentor's murderous son, *Mo-sheel*.[10]

It has been written, and generally accepted as fact, that Bolon was pursued and overtaken by *Mo-*

17

sheel and his party. The contrary, according to *Su-el-lil*, was the case. Bolon, *Su-el-lil* asserts, overtook the Indians who had no knowledge of his presence in the country until he appeared.

It also has been claimed—and not disputed until recent years—that *Qual-chan*, the fierce warrior nephew of Chief *Ka-mi-a-kun*, was the instigator of the murder and the leading perpetrator. And *Ka-mi-a-kun* himself has been charged with being privy to it. Neither [one] was anywhere in the neighborhood nor knew anything about it until after the crime had been committed. But, when Colonel George Wright, at the close of his successful campaign in the Spokane country in 1858, hanged *Qual-chan*—as he did many captive chiefs and warriors—he believed that the summary execution ended the career of the "villain" responsible for Bolon's slaying.

The Reverend Stwire G. Waters, Klikitat full-blood, minister of the Methodist Episcopal church, and chief of the Yakima Indian confederation, supplied McWhorter with interesting bits about the principals of the Bolon affair.

Waters, as a youth, was a pupil in the Jason Lee missionary school near Salem, in the Willamette Valley. He was ordained a Methodist minister in Portland in 1871, and was made an elder of the church at Moscow, Idaho, in 1888. His labor for the church, he always said, was due to the influence of the Reverend James H. Wilbur, the famed "Father Wilbur," Methodist missionary and Oregon territory pioneer, who served as Indian school superintendent on the Yakima reservation from 1860 to 1864, and for nearly twenty years after that as Indian agent of the Yakimas. The Reverend Waters was elected head chief of the Yakima Confederation on March 22, 1910. He died some years ago.

In discussing the Bolon tragedy with McWhorter in 1916, Chief Waters said:

"*Mo-sheel* was the son of *Show-a-wai Ko-ti-a-ken*, who was a brother of Chief *Ka-mi-a-kun* and of the Paloos tribe.[11] The mother of *Mo-sheel* was a Yakima; and his wife, *Ceates*, was a Klikitat. Both *Mo-sheel* and his father were tall, well-built men. I remember them well.

Mo-sheel attended the Methodist mission school (Jason Lee school) a few miles southwest of where Oregon City now stands. He went there soon after the establishment of the mission in 1836. I saw him in Vancouver in 1851 [sic]. He had run away from school in 1852 [sic] and never went back. He was spare, sinewy and quick in movement. His people for generations had been warriors, and he, himself, was a wild young man.

I saw Mr. Bolon at Vancouver. He was a tall, large man, had red hair and wore a beard. He was very athletic and fond of sport. In the spring of 1853 he ran a race on foot against the race horse of Chief *Tom-i-tash*, at Vancouver, where there were only soldiers, Hudson's Bay Company people, and Klikitats. The race was fifty yards. He won against the horse, beating it by about twelve feet. I saw this race. Bolon was a great friend of the Klikitats.[12]

Mr. Bolon came to the Yakima country to counsel with the Indians. Then he started on his return to The Dalles. He was never seen again by either friendly Indians or whites. I always understood that he was killed by the young men and that the old men knew nothing about it until it was all over.

"I did not know that Yakima George *(Su-el-lil)* was with *Mo-sheel's* party. I guess he was afraid and kept it hid. He was old enough at that time to go hunting, for he is the same age as myself, and I am seventy-six. He is a truthful man, and would not lie to you. If he said he was along, then he was there. I never talked to him about it."

Major Jay Lynch, who had been superintendent of the Yakima Reservation for a score of years, in response to an inquiry by McWhorter, unhesitatingly declared:

"I have known Yakima George now for twenty-three years, and all through my incumbency as superintendent of the Yakima Agency, I had dealings with him as a ward of the government, and can say with genuine candor that I always found him truthful and scrupulously honest in his every statement and business deals. I would not for a moment doubt his recital as an eyewitness to the Bolon tragedy as he gave it to you. You need have no hesitancy in making historical use of his story."

H.D.G.

At the October 6, 1918, dedication of the marker at the murder site of Indian Agent Major Andrew J. Bolon; L-r: L.V. McWhorter; William Charley and wife; William Bonney, Secty., Washington State Historical Society, Tacoma. Photo courtesy of Washington State Historical Society, Tacoma, WA.

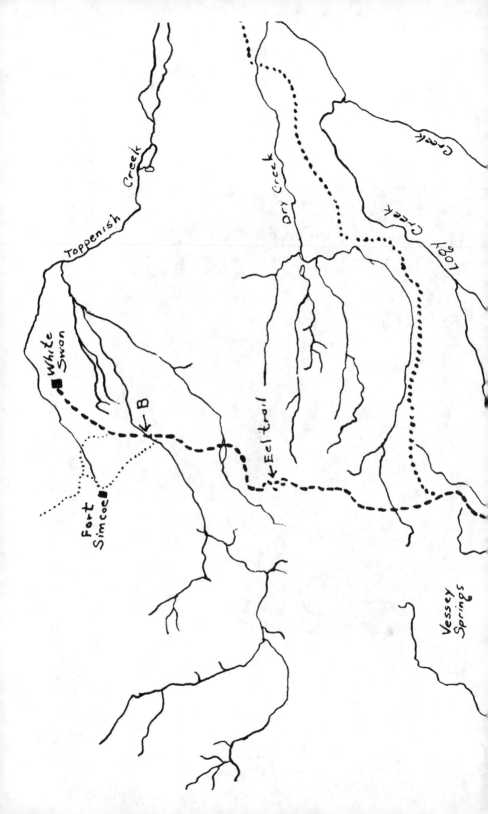

Legend:
- ▬▬▬ Trail from Yakima Country to Cello Fo (Bolon turned back at "B")
- ⋯⋯⋯ Indian Trails
- ●●● Wee-tal-e-kec (Dry Creek) trail
- ┌┘┐ Present day roads
- ✗ Marker at Walk-Shum Spring (Bolon killed here)
- M Bolon Monument

Scale of miles
1 2 3 4 5 6

N
W —┼— E
S

Salax

Boundary

Reservation

Marker

Monument

Goldendale

To Cello Falls

The small boulder at the Indian's feet marks the spot where the Indians built their campfire. Bolon was standing just to the north of the fire when attacked, killed. This photo, looking southeast, was made by L.V. McWhorter, 26 Aug 1917. Photo courtesy of Washington State Historical Society, Tacoma, WA.

III. THE KILLING OF
MAJOR BOLON

As Told by *Su-el-lil*—Eyewitness;
John Billie (1911) and William Charley (1915),
Interpreters

What I am telling you happened before the war with the soldiers. It was about the close of huckleberry time [September?].

The Indians had returned from the mountains, and our party was on its way to The Dalles to get dried salmon. We went from Dry Creek, on the Yakima Reservation, over the *Wee-tal-e-kee*[13] Trail. The first night we camped at a place called *Yah-hoh*[14] where there are two trails. One of these follows along a small stream by which we stopped. It rained hard all night. It was cold and chilly.

Next morning we started on the trail--six men, several women and myself, a boy. I do not know my exact age, but I know within a year or so. I must have been about fourteen years old at that time, for I remember everything well. I cared for the horses on that trip, and I often went with my father, hunting. I was a strong boy with the rifle.

TRAGEDY OF THE *WAHK-SHUM*

That morning *Wah-tah-kon* left early to hunt *yah-mas* [mule deer] near where a sawmill now [1911] stands. The rest of us traveled on the *Weetal-e-kee* Trail until the sun was about there [indicating around ten o'clock], when we entered the *Ah-soom*[15] Trail which comes over from the upper *Thap-pahn-ish.*[16] Soon we saw a man going on this trail, coming after us. He overtook us before we got to the summit of the *Wahk-shum* Mountain. He was white. I had never seen a White person before. He rode a gray horse, and he came over the *Ah-soom* from near *Mool-Mool.*[17] He came up with us at or near *We-twash taw-us.*[18]

Chief *Mo-sheel* was at the head of our party. He knew the White man, and he told the other Indians who he was.

The white man said, "Hello, *Mo-sheel.*"

I understand but little English, but I know now that was what he said. He had seen *Mo-sheel* at the Willamette school.

Then Chief *Mo-sheel* shook hands with the stranger, and, while the women kept on the trail, all the other men shook hands with him.

The White man was large, not very fleshy, and had a reddish beard. He was a strong looking man.

Chief *Mo-sheel* spoke to his people: "This is the man who hanged my uncles and cousins at Wallula."[19] *Mo-sheel* knew him and was mad.

Then we traveled. Chief *Mosheel*, Captain *Wah-pi-wah-pi-lah*, a powerfully strong man, and *So-qiekt* [or *So-kiat*] rode in front with the White man;

THE KILLING OF MAJOR BOLON

one and one they rode on the trail. *Nou-yan-nan* [or *Nou-yan-en*], *Stah-kin* [or *Sta-chen*], and I, *Su-el-lil*, fell in behind. While going, *Mo-sheel* and *Wah-pi-wah-pi-lah* wanted to kill the White man, but *Nou-yah-nan* opposed. *Mo-sheel* insisted. He was angry because the White man had hanged his kin. He said, "I am going to kill him the same as he killed my poor people."

We who were behind did not know. We came on fast; it was cold and raining hard. We went on down the trail on *Wahk-shum* Mountain [Simcoe Mountain] across a little stream running down the mountain. Someone said, "We shall not make fire here. We will make it at the spring below, at *Wahk-shum*."

We went fast and stopped at the spring and made a fire--a big fire, lots of fire, for we were very wet and cold.

The White man unbridled his horse so he could eat, took a lunch rolled and tied to the back of his saddle, and came to the fire. He left his *canteenis* [saddlebags] and six-shooter in its holster on the saddle. We were all standing about the fire, warming [ourselves]. The White man pulled off his overcoat; he had on an undercoat. He stood with us, holding his hands to the flames, warming by the big fire.

The women had gone on down the trail; they did not stop. Chief *Mo-sheel's* wife, *Ceates*, was with them. She was a good woman, and died not many years ago [1905].

Then the White man took his lunch and di-

TRAGEDY OF THE *WAHK-SHUM*

vided it with the Indians.

Stah-kin stepped about twelve feet from the fire. *Wah-pi-wah-pilah* now said to his son-in-law, *Stah-kin*, "*Mo-sheel* wants to kill the White man."

Stah-kin tried to keep him from it. He told *Nou-yah-nan* of the plot. *Nou-yah-nan* was an old man, and he said:

No! We will get into trouble. Let him alone. All at headquarters at *Wal-lo-la* [Wallula] know of this White man. Do not kill him; all will be trouble."

Mo-sheel said, "You are not chief. I am chief. I will kill this man, as he killed my brothers. I thought to meet him some time, and now I have met him this day. I will kill him." 20

The White man stood, holding his hands up to the fire. *Wah-pi-wah-pi-lah* stood by him on the left. Chief *Mo-sheel* stood on his right.

"We [had] better hurry," somebody said.

I did not know what was up. I was eating hardtack which the White man had given to me.

Chief *Mo-sheel* again spoke to *Wah-pi--wah-pi-lah*, "We better hurry!"

Then *Wah-pi-wah-pi-lah*, the strong man, dropped quickly and caught the white man by the legs and jerked him to the ground. *So-qiekt* and *Mo-sheel* jumped on him, each catching an arm, *Mo-sheel* on the right. The white man cried out [in Chinook]:

"Do not kill me! I did not come to fight you!"

I did not then understand Chinook, but that is what I always understood that he said.

28

THE KILLING OF MAJOR BOLON

Stah-kin grabbed his beard, pulled back his head, and called: "Hurry!"

So-qiekt threw him a knife, and *Stah-kin* cut the White man's throat. He struggled a short time and then lay still, the blood running from the big knife wound. He was dead.

I ran around, squealing.

Nou-yah-nan, the old man, sat at the fire and said nothing. Chief *Mo-sheel* spoke to him, "If you do not keep quiet, I will kill you."

Then they caught the White man's horse and said "We will kill him also."

Nou-yah-nan now spoke, "No use to kill the horse. Keep all that the White man had."

But they did not listen. They stripped the saddle from the horse and placed the dead man on his own saddle blanket. They took off his coat and vest and one pair of pantaloons or overalls. He had on one other pair, also [a] shirt and underclothing. These they did not take from him; neither did they take his hat. They carried him away on the blanket, leading his horse. They went down about a quarter of a mile from the camp where a pine tree had turned out by the roots. They placed him in this cavity, put his overcoat on him, and covered him with the saddle blanket. Then they threw dirt, broken limbs, and brush on him.

I did not see this, but I was always told that was the way that they buried him. While this was being done, I sat at the fire with *Nou-yah-nan*. We heard the shot that killed the horse--good white [gray] horse.[21]

TRAGEDY OF THE *WAHK-SHUM*

The Indians came back to the camp. They divided the goods belonging to the White man. Chief *Mo-sheel* took his six-shooter, holster and *canteenis* [saddlebags]. *Stah-kin* got one blanket, and *So-qiekt* the other one. *Wah-pi-wah-pi-lah* took his coat, vest, and the one pair of pantaloons. The saddle was concealed until the party returned from The Dalles, when they took it away with them. I do not know what was done with the bridle. I did not see any money or other things which the White man may have had about him.

After my father, *Wah-tah-kon*, rejoined the party from his *yah-mas* hunt and learned what had been done, he upbraided the warriors and told them that they had done a bad thing, and that there would be trouble. He nearly had a fight with *Wah-pi-wah-pi-lah* who was a great strong man.[22] *Wah-tah-kon* had killed one *yah-mas*.

My father left the party, taking me and his women folks with him. When he got to [now] Fall Bridge, he reported the killing to the Whites.[23]

I never heard that the body of the White man was ever recovered. I always understood that it was not. I can now go to the exact spot where he was killed.

The warriors who killed this White man all fought in the war which followed.

So-qiekt shot and killed himself after the war closed and the Indians had lost out.

Chief *Mo-sheel*, *Wah-pi-wah-pi-lah*, and *Stah-- kin* [after the war] were in a tepee on the lower Satus amusing themselves--gambling. *Wantah*, a Klikitat Indian known as *Wan-to*, carried the news to *Mool--mool* [Fort Simcoe]; and soldiers, guided by *Wan-tah*, surprised them and surrounded the tepee.

Chief *Mo-sheel* attempted to escape by running, and was shot through the belly and shoulder. *Wan-tah*, it was said, sent the bullet through his belly that caused his death.

Wah-pi-wah-pi-lah and *Stah-kin* were captured in the tepee and afterwards hanged at *Mool-mool*.[24]

The soldiers carried Chief *Mo-sheel* on a blanket to, or near *Thap-pahn-ish* lake where he died. He had died [become unconscious] twice while being carried; and the soldiers, not believing he was dead, built sagebrush fires on both sides of him and burned him some to see if he was really dead. His body was taken to *Mool-mool* and given to his people.

Some say that *Mo-sheel* was carried tied across a horse, and, when he died and was partly burned, was left by the soldiers for the coyotes, and that his sister found his body and buried it.

Chief *Mo-sheel's* wife was *Ceates*, and she was along with the other six women when the White man was killed on the *Ah-soom* Trail.

His son, Chief *Yoom-tee-bee*, was not born until soon after the killing.[25] Chief *Mo-sheel* was the son of Chief *Show-a-wai Ko-ti-a-ken*.

Nou-yan-nan died many years afterward near the Indian race track, some two miles southeast of

TRAGEDY OF THE *WAHK-SHUM*

where White Swan now stands.

Wah-tah-kon, my father, was thrown from a horse some fifteen years later and killed at Klikitat, between Goldendale and Centerville, Washington. This is all.

WAH-TAH-KON'S PROPHECY

It is said that *Wah-tah-kon* possessed a very strong *Tah* [mystery power], which endowed him with a remarkable prophetic vision, not wholly unlike the "second sight" of the Scottish Highlanders of old.

William Charley says that *Wah-tan-kon*, at the morning repast on the fateful day of Bolon's murder, warned his fellow campers with the following startling revelation:

"Last night in my waking-sleep I saw a White man. I know not how I saw him, but he was there before my eyes as I now see you. Blood was upon him! He was all stained with blood! Blood on his face; blood on his clothes. He was not good to see. Listen well to my words; what I am telling you! If you do not, you will know sorrow. Trouble will follow and overtake you on the trail.

"Should you see a White man today, if you meet one, do not bother him. Do him no harm. Let him alone to go his own way, to live his own life. Put no blood upon him. You will bring evil to our lives if you do. Remember what I am telling you."

IV. LOCATING THE SCENE OF
THE BOLON TRAGEDY

After *Su-el-lil*, sometimes pronounced *Sui-lil*-possibly a corruption of *Sar-el-lil*, a family that resided in the Kittitas Valley—had told his story, he agreed to act as pilot to the scene of the Bolon tragedy, providing that his son-in-law, William Charley, would go as interpreter. But there were many delays, and not until November, 1915, could arrangements be effected for the trip.

We met at the home of *Listening Coyote*, a half-blood, known to the Whites as Simon Goudy, near White Swan the morning of November 8. I [L. V. McWhorter] had ridden to Simon's place the day before on a horse borrowed from one of *Su-el-lil's* Indian neighbors south of Toppenish.

Snow fell that night, and lowering, leaden clouds in the morning presaged more of it. Simon endeavored to discourage the trip, experienced mountain man that he was.

"Can't you see what you are running into?" he admonished. "No man has any business going into those mountains this time of year without a tent, blankets and plenty of both grub and horse feed. At least two pack horses are needed for a party of three, but you have none. No! Not even a blanket, much less a shelter tent." "Yesterday," he continued, "I was up the trail twelve miles getting wood. There were four inches of snow. More fell last night, and more is coming. It will be deeper where you are going, and much colder. Didn't you hear the coyotes last night? How unusually prolonged their howling was? If [you are] as wise as they, you will stay close to shelter. A storm is gathering, and I know what that means in the higher range where you have to cross going and returning. But you may get lost and never return. Take my advice; do not go."

I replied that if the trip was given up, it never would be made; that on prior occasions arrangements for going had fallen through; that *Su-el-lil*, who had seen seventy-five snows, was riding thirty miles to keep his promise—that he doubtless could not be induced to make a later attempt. It was now or never.

"Then let it be never, for that is what it will amount to if you do not return," Simon declared impatiently. "If you go, you are sure to remember what I have told you."

But the die was cast; and when Mrs. Goudy was asked for a lunch for the trip, two biscuits, a very small piece of sausage and a slice of jerked venison was all that she could rake together. Expressing regret at being unable to provide more, she handed the packet

LOCATING THE MURDER SITE

to me and spoke with great solicitude, "Big Foot [the Indians' nickname for L.V. McWhorter] will be lost in the mountain storms and not come back. We will never more see him."

Her words were to be remembered under conditions not dreamed of.

Approaching the shed where my horse was quartered, I overheard Listening Coyote lamenting to his colored helper.

"McWhorter," he was saying, "has no business going. He is already 'barkin'' with a cold. I know where they are headed for, and I know what the weather will be. I do not like it. I wish he would not go. He does not realize what danger he is running into."

Su-el-lil and William Charley, well mounted, finally arrived.

Simon, who had concluded it was useless to urge further against our going, donated three pecks of oats with the observation, "The poor horses should not be made to suffer because of their crazy owners. They will need more, but this is enough extra weight to carry in back of your saddles."

The sun, which was shining faintly when we started, was soon blotted out. By noon we reached Simon's wood camp at a distance of twelve miles from his house, and there allowed the horses to feed on sparse hay scattered about and half buried in the snow. After a half hour rest we were off again. The trail grew rougher, and many detours around fallen timber and

TRAGEDY OF THE *WAHK-SHUM*

snow-covered branches were necessary.

By midafternoon the divide between Dry Creek and Brush Creek on the summit between the headwaters of Dry Creek and Brush Creek, the divisional watershed of the Satus River and Cedar Valley region, had been attained. Several fresh trails made by wild horses leaving the forest for the lower country—a bad omen for us—were noted. They were getting out before snow blocked the summit, and made it impassable for the next six months. Places of interest were pointed out by the Indians. It was here, on the divide of the two creeks, that *Su-el-lil* and *Wha-mish*, another medicine man, narrowly escaped death many years before. With William Charley interpreting, *Su-el-lil* told about it as we rode along.

"It was this same time of year," he said, "that we were returning from Celilo Falls, above the Dalles, with dried salmon. A bad storm overtook us at this very spot, and we were stalled. Here, the wind does not sweep across the ridge. It does not go anywhere. It stays here. Whirling, it twists up clouds of snow, and you cannot see anything. You cannot make your horses go. The dark air cuts like whips. It was freezing cold. We could not build a fire. The storm roared. We talked only by shouting to each other, staying close together. We were held here two days. When the storm stopped, we had just one pack horse left; the other three and our saddle horses were dead—buried under a great drift of snow. We made snowshoes before getting out from here."

LOCATING THE MURDER SITE

To this cheerful narrative William grimly added: "We are more than likely to meet just such a storm on our way back. A *Chil-wit* (bad) spirit rules here. Only in late spring, in summer and late autumn, is it safe traveling this pass. He does not bother you then, but not so this time of year. He lets you go through, but lays for you on your return."

It had begun to snow, and we rode on in silence. Soon it was snowing furiously, and, for that reason, *Su-el-lil* objected to striking off on the trail over which Major Bolon traveled to his death sixty years before. No longer an Indian thoroughfare, it was choked with a growth of young pine, and now was practically impassable, due to wet, soggy snow loading the small trees. So, we continued on the newer trail, a rough wagon road, heading for the Indian Service forest station at Vessey Springs. We got there at dusk and expected to find a comfortable night's shelter.

A roaring log fire had been pictured in the great open fireplace, but the building was found securely locked and barred against intrusion.

There was a small, floorless outbuilding with a narrow open shed adjoining. Crowding our horses into the room, we fed them some of the oats that Listening Coyote had supplied, and made ourselves as comfortable as possible. A fire was built, a very small one that would not set the roof ablaze over our heads, and about it we hovered.

As my companions made no move toward lunching, I proceeded with pencil and tablet to verify

TRAGEDY OF THE *WAHK-SHUM*

certain parts of *Su-el-lil's* Bolon narrative that were
not entirely clear. It was nine o'clock before this was
finished.

Presently, *Su-el-lil* spoke to William, who
smilingly explained: "The old man is hungry and
wants to know when we are going to eat."

Explaining that I had been waiting for them to
begin, and was wondering why they had not done so,
William sprang surprise by announcing that they had
not brought any food, depending upon me to furnish it.
I displayed my meager store, and explained why so
little. They both laughed as if the joke was more on me
than on themselves, and we divided the lunch. William and I each had half of one biscuit, and *Su-el-lil* the
other biscuit.

Then we 'turned in.' I had neither blanket nor
overcoat. William had a blanket but no coat; while *Su-
el-lil*, wise in years and experience, had brought along
an overcoat and two blankets. I removed spurs, but
kept on a heavy mackinaw and canvas puttees. Spread-
ing a thirty-six by forty-eight inch canvas for bedding,
a short saddle blanket for covering, and a saddle for
pillow, the night was spent in semi-comfort.

As we had no breakfast to bother with in the
morning, it did not take long to get started after giving
a ration of oats to the horses. The bulk of the remaining
oats was cached, with just enough retained for an
ordinary feed for each horse, for we planned to return
there that evening.

We had not ridden far when snow began falling. Big, soggy flakes!

Slight the day before, my cold now seemed to be developing into a bad case of lung congestion, and I grew uneasy. To get relief, deep inhaling and exhaling were practiced at short intervals the greater part of the forenoon. The exercise effected a complete cure. This remedy has been tried since then, and under far more favorable conditions with no beneficial results. Its "magic" had flown.

Getting down into Cedar valley, we arrived at a cabin clearing, one of the several white homesteads within the Yakima reservation.[26] Passing it, the Goldendale road was struck just below Baker's sawmill; and at a rancher's cabin two small loaves of bread were obtained from the housewife. She lamented that the sponge had soured, and the bread [was] thereby heavy and soggy. But we were glad to have it.

The storm was increasing, with a bitter wind shipping from the north; we did not pause to eat, but pushed up a hill to the left of the cabin and into the forest.

Su-el-lil was certain that at no great distance we would come to the old trail "where the White man was killed."

It is well to say here that I had but a vague idea of the cardinal points and actual distances between turns in our route, never having been in the region; and, owing to the storm, [our] range of vision was limited. We had no compass.

Su-el-lil had described the place of the killing

as an "open-like park," with larger trees than in the surrounding forest.

Proceeding up a wagon trail for two or three miles, we came to a small area answering the old Indian's description. The trees were large and scattered. *Su-el-lil* said that there seemed to be more undergrowth than when he had last seen it fifty years before. And William explained that small growth and trees had sprung up on all the abandoned trails, and had obliterated many of them through those mountains. However, this holds good throughout the timbered regions which fact should rejoice all lovers of the forest wilds.

After a critical scrutiny of the park, *Su-el-lil* pointed to one side and said he was sure there was the spot we sought. If correct, he declared, the trail on which he and his party traveled that fateful day in 1855 would be found crossing through a gap or pass in a bare ridge which loomed ahead of us. On either side of the trail, at the summit, he said, would be a small heap of stones. He wanted to go up there, so we rode out of the sheltering timber and up the long, exposed slope over which the rising wind drove a downpour of swirling snow.

In the pass the snow lay deep, and all traces of any trail there, and the guiding cairns—which were later estimated about three inches in height—were hidden. But on the ascent traces of the old trail had been noted; and taking bearings from two prominent bald knobs, *Su-el-lil* announced that he had made no

LOCATING THE MURDER SITE

mistake: that where he pointed out down in the park was where the White man had died.

These observations were being made from the saddle, when my horse suddenly went down in apparent exhaustion. Afoot!—and the vision of a long, back trail loomed darkly! But somber reckoning was broken into by William's sharp admonition:

"*Su-el-lil* says hurry if we are to stop and mark the place. He says we will mark it, then get out from here fast. He fears a storm on the mountain pass like the one he told us about yesterday. He thinks it may be too late already to get there in daylight; and if we do not make it before night, we never will. Evil of any kind is more evil in darkness."

I knew that we had described, roughly, a half-circle in our traveling, and that we probably had covered forty miles from the pass on the divide between Dry and Brush Creeks—pass of bad repute.

"William!"—I spoke against the roar of the wind—"we can never make that pass before dark. It is now 10 o'clock, and you see the condition of my horse. Let the marking go! We know the place. Don't you know some way north from here?"

William said that he could, that he would steer for a landmark we had passed on the trail the day before. *Su-el-lil* agreeing to this arrangement, we headed northward. I led my horse for some time, until we came to the timber again, and then got back in the saddle. William rode ahead to break the trail. I was next, and *Su-el-lil* last. Riding in this order, much of the snow was dislodged from branches along the trail, making it easier for our companion.

About midday we came to a frightfully steep descent, perhaps an eighth of a mile down, bare of timber but thatched with shrubs in places. Since William said there was no way around, we struck down the slope. It proved a veritable slide of volcanic rock, dangerous enough in good weather, and terribly so with the covering snow. Upon reaching the bottom, we found it gorged completely with huge boulders and fallen timber. There was nothing to do but retrace our way. I led my horse, but not so the Indians. I have yet to see an Indian dismount because of the roughness of the trail.

William was well up the slide, and I was a couple of rods ahead of *Su-el-lil*, when the latter's horse stumbled and fell in the roughest of the rocks. Turning at the unusual racket, I saw the horse regain its feet, and *Su-el-lil* struggling amid the boulders and the snow. Leaving my horse, I hurried to help him, and was greatly relieved to find him unhurt. He made no comment, spoke not a word, as, with my aid, he slowly gained the top of the bluff where William awaited with our horses. After a short rest and council we re-mounted and set out again, but of the cardinal direction, none of us knew. In the driving snow vision was limited to half of a city block. Because of his defective vision, *Su-el-lil* ventured no advice. Disconcerted by the forced digression from his course, William was visibly confused.

LOCATING THE MURDER SITE

We were lost. William was guiding solely by guess. The erratic wind, buffeting us at all angles, afforded no clue as to cardinal points. We were a badly discouraged trio; and our horses, had they been endowed with human speech, doubtless would have revealed a like state of mind.

For about an hour we held to what William thought a northerly course, slow plodding, with the wind blowing more chill all the time. Occasionally *Su-el-lil* would ejaculate:

"*Wake siah memaloose!*—"Death is not far (away)!"

Then he would chuckle, as if in ironical amusement.

At last William remarked that he was at a loss which way to turn. We were in an old "burn" where the dead tree trunks had been divested of all limbs except on one side. His attention was called to the fact that the limbs probably had been stripped off by the wind, and that, since the prevailing gales were from the northwest, the remaining branch-stubs must be pointing southeast. Taking his bearings accordingly, William again led off in what we thought a northerly direction. The snow let up slightly. We had proceeded for another hour when we came to a trail freshly made, winding off to our left, apparently the general course that we wanted to go. For myself, this harbinger of hope was hailed with inward delight. William said nothing until within a rod of the broken snow; then he reined his horse to a sudden stop, with a grim exclama-

TRAGEDY OF THE *WAHK-SHUM*

tion:

"*Bygod*! We are lost!"

"*Wake siah memmaloose!*" was *Su-el-lil's* chuckling response.

We had circled and were back on our own trail.

William delivered a mild (?) reprimand for my bringing them on such a trip at that season of the year, which ended in a brief and serious council. At its conclusion the snow-trail was crossed at right angles, and our forlorn groping resumed. William was chanting an invocatory "medicine" song which he presently interrupted to mutter:

"After this all the godam ossifers can get killed for me."

By midafternoon we came upon a rotting, tumble-down Indian shack, and stopped to feed horses and ourselves. The animals were led inside; their oats were poured on top of a rusty, pipeless cook stove, while we ate bread standing. When starting again, we were cheered somewhat by a lifting of the storm and the appearance of the sun, which hung low over the western horizon. It revealed that instead of north we had wandered widely southeast. Taking his bearings, William volunteered:

"I know where we are, and it is a long way off the trail we have been trying to find. Over there," pointing to a long ridge to the east, "is where *Santos* killed the deer. We will go there and try to reach lower ground where dry wood for night camping can be found. *Su-el-lil* says that he is very tired and cold."

LOCATING THE MURDER SITE

Turning in his saddle, William pointed to a mountain whose rugged slope gleamed in the sun. "There," he explained, "is where the old man came near being killed."

It was true. Our zigzag trail was there plainly visible; even to the wallowed out spot where *Su-el-lil's* horse went down, which William solemnly maintained was my *footprint*. I was puzzled! When that trail was in the making, the mountain faced due west; but it was now looking squarely to the sunrise.

With revived hopes we headed east and made fair progress, considering the tangle of fallen timber and dense, young pine growth to be contended with. But this did not last. The sun again became obscured. About sundown we stumbled onto the ruins of an ancient, Indian horse corral and a remnant of barbed wire fence. I dismounted to press down a rusty strand of the wire so the horses could cross; and before I could get back in the saddle, William spoke in a startling, hurried tone:

"Get on your hoss quick!—let's get out from here! Coming the worst storm yet."

Glancing roundabout, the sight was appalling. There can be no word description. Boiling tumultuously up from every side was a seething, blue-black ring, contracting and advancing at terrific speed. A comparison to the blue wave which spreads over hot steel in process of tempering flashed through my mind. A moment later we seemed to stand on the highest and only visible ground in the world, with a billowy,

45

TRAGEDY OF THE *WAHK-SHUM*

vapory ocean heaving wildly upward and about us. *Su-el-lil*, sitting on his horse, with tragically outstretched arm, voiced his ever solemn, prophetic warning:

"*Yuka delate sollex! Wake siah memaloose!*" (He is very angry. Death is not far.) Nor was the usual embellishing laugh wanting.

I am sure now that none of us at that moment held serious hope of ever leaving that tangled desolation alive. The poetic grandeur of the venerable Klikitat's philosophic, *Dreamer* acceptance of the inevitable was sublimely uplifting. It plainly said: "Live your life; have your fling; then go without murmur when the call comes."

Hastily mounting we were again off; plunged into the darkest, dankest cloud-smother that one could well imagine; a blackened gloom driven by a furious gale, ladened with stinging pellets of icy snow. This precipitation, if continued for any time, would form a hard, cutting crust which we knew our horses would refuse to "buck."

Increasing darkness warned of approaching night, and William and myself kept a sharp watch for possible fire material. The only semblance to likely fuel observed was a two-foot snag projecting from a fallen tree trunk, at the edge of the timberline as we emerged on a barren, desert ridge. I reached down and broke it off and carried it along to have in case nothing better was found. The wind had not abated, and the "*crunch, crunch*" of our horse's feet revealed the

LOCATING THE MURDER SITE

forming of the dreaded snow crust.

William suddenly pulled up and pointed, saying, "I see a light away off there. It must be a sheep camp! Had we better try making it?"

I could discern no light, but answered that we should make the attempt; to stop where we were would be fatal.

"Yes," he replied, "the old man says that he is growing numb, and I know that he cannot stand much more of this."

As we moved silently on, the familiar "*Wake siah memaloose*," with its accompanying chuckle perceptibly weaker, was ominously prophetic.

The distant light disappeared. William said it was possibly obscured by an intervening peak or forest. The cold was growing more intense, and the startling audibility attending on every step of our mounts told too well the growing thickness of the chafing snow crust. After, as near as could be surmised, two or three miles of painful progress, the *will-o-the-wisp* light reappeared. This time I could distinguish it, a mere twinkle, apparently miles and miles away, hanging in chaos. The whole world seemed a rimless void save the spot on which we stood. We had not advanced one hundred yards when the beacon was blotted out not to be seen again. The chuckle accompanying the *Wake siah memaloose* at this stage was like a grim jest.

A rift in the clouds—the storm was subsiding. A weak moon and a few stars shed a dim light.

TRAGEDY OF THE *WAHK-SHUM*

Changing our course, we soon entered a deep wood, and started down the mountain, which shielded us from the yet unsettled gale. In the gloom was perceived a cluster of dead willows, and investigation disclosed an abundance of dry fuel—poles, some of them alder—standing and prone. I shouted to William, who was exploring ahead; brought him back; and we helped *Su-el-lil* from his horse.

Gathering dry twigs and moss from the trunk of a large pine nearby, match after match was touched to this tinder without effect. Remembering a fragment of newspaper in my saddle pockets, it was ignited with the last match, and a tinder blaze was started. Never did fire seem so good.

William prepared to use the great pine as a back wall for our fire. Always a worshipper of trees, I mildly suggested that the pine be spared, but such sentiment was overruled. William's contention that the lives of "three Injuns" should not be risked for the sake of a solitary tree in that great forest prevailed, and soon cheery flames were roaring against the upper side of it.

By kicking and scraping away the snow, we secured a fairly dry spot for bedding down. Close to this, the horses were tethered that they might derive some benefit from the heat. Hungry as they were, their scant remaining oat ration was withheld until morning. My horse was blanketed with the piece of canvas which had protected my knees during the day's ride. By comradeship rights, it was his for the night.

LOCATING THE MURDER SITE

Su-el-lil, accorded central place at the fire, reclined on his blanket and sipped at a bit of snow. Utterly exhausted, he gazed silently at the dancing flames. William and I stood, drying our clothes and comparing notes. He had kept fairly dry, with his heavy-napped Hudson's Bay blanket, worn only as an Indian can drape. "Ice bergs" had formed in the fingertips of my canvas gloves, but, strange to say, with no deleterious results. The protective value of hair reaching well down over the coat collar in such weather was attested by the fringe of ice clinging thereto. William, noticing our steaming clothes, laconically remarked:

"You will thaw out next May, if the wolves and coyotes don't find you." And then, "You are the first man ever to come into these mountains at this time of year. All the Indians know the danger and stay away. You took all this chance with death just to know where one man was killed who came into the Indian country looking for trouble. You had no business bringing us on such a dangerous trip. If we die out here, if we do not get back home, it will be your fault. *Su-el-lil* said he wanted to go last July, but you did not seem to think it a good time."

"Yes," I explained, "he did speak to me at the Fourth of July Indian gathering at *Thap-pahn-ish*, but we wanted you as interpreter; and you were not there. I did not know the danger of going at this time of year, but you did. Why were you silent? Why did you not refuse to go?"

TRAGEDY OF THE *WAHK-SHUM*

His reply was a hark back to the primitive Indian's concept of his word of honor. "We had promised you to go!"

We ate the last of our bread. *Su-el-lil* offered me one of his blankets, which Indian etiquette presumed should be accepted. But I could not permit his sacrifice, and declined with apology for the seeming discourtesy.

The Indians slept that night. I catnapped and kept the fire going.

The morning dawned clear and quiet, with only a few clouds to remind us of the fury of the storm. William announced that we were in Satus canyon which, he said, he had surmised the evening before. He said we should continue on the same course, and would strike the high tableland of the reservation, between the Satus, Logie and Dry Creeks. We had traveled miles out of our way. But a benign star had guided us to the only tinder wood of the day's rambling; and that, too, as daylight was to reveal, at the very brink of a great slant which, had we struck it in darkness, doubtless would have been disastrous to one or all.

Feeding the last of the oats to the horses, we mounted. We had not gone fifty yards until we came to the brow of a steep declivity that extended to the bottom of the gorge far below. The Indians engaged in an earnest colloquy.

"What is wrong, William?" I asked.

"The old man does not want to go down this

50

steep place. He is afraid. He wants to go around."

I confess that I did not relish the prospective descent either, but, when William said it was that or to go back the way we came, an ordeal that the horses could not have stood, I said we should go on. William informed *Su-el-lil* that it was wholly impractical to turn back, that we would have to make the descent at all hazards, adding—as he afterward told me—"I am young and can easily make it home even if my horse is killed or crippled. I will leave you both unless you come on"— beautiful liar that he was.

So, into the yawning depths we descended. The Indians stayed on their horses. I led mine. Slow and precarious, but the venture was without accident. At the bottom men and horses had water for the first time after leaving Vessey's Springs. The climb out of the canyon was arduous but not so steep as the way into it. The sun was brilliant when the top was gained. A bear had left his trail in the snow, and William remarked that he would "get that bear" during the winter. Riding out on the bunch grass tableland, he pointed to the southeast and declared that the "mystery" fire we had seen the evening before was "over there in the Bickleton country, fifteen miles away."

But I could not figure out how that could possibly be. It was in an exactly opposite direction when I noted it.

At noon we arrived at a sheep camp, where, in accordance with a recognized "law of the range," we cooked and ate hungrily, not forgetting to leave pans and skillet cleaned, and a note of thanks for the absent herder. The famished horses in the meantime had been busy filling up on straw scattered about the camp, and they, too, felt better as we lined out on a lope across the open country. We were crossing the high tablelands of the Yakima Indian reservation.

It was about thirty-five miles to Toppenish where a train could be caught at six o'clock for Yakima. William explained this to *Su-el-lil*, who said: "We will ride fast all the time, and ride hard part of the time, and make it." We had left the snowline at the summit of the Satus ridge.

Ten miles from the sheep camp, William left us to strike north to White Swan. *Su-el-lil* and I pressed on steadily, alternately at a trot and a gallop. We saw some of the only remaining bunch of sage hens on the reservation, and in the distance two or three bands of wild horses that had been driven from the mountain wilderness by the storm which was so nearly our undoing.

Darkness overtook us several miles out of Toppenish, but, by maintaining our brisk pace, we were at the outskirts of the town when the train whistled for the station. I caught the train with two minutes to spare. The strange part of the story of that ride is that the Indian cayuse showed no symptoms of playing out despite his display of fatigue the previous day in the mountains.

Although *Su-el-lil* had stood the trip with a fortitude becoming a much younger man, the rigors of

LOCATING THE MURDER SITE

it hastened his decline.

When George H. Himes, secretary of the Oregon Pioneer Association, heard of our trip, he wanted a group photograph of the three of us for historical record. William interpreting, this was explained to *Su-el-lil* late in the summer of 1916. He listened attentively, deliberated, and said:

"All the long snows I kept secret that I saw the White man killed. William Charley, my son-in-law, was the only Indian I ever told it to. This is how you came to know and to ask me for the story. I was glad to give it to you as true history; yet, all the time I was afraid to talk. I might be hanged. I am glad I pointed out to you where the White man was killed. But that trip was too much for my winters.

"You ask for my picture for history. I will tell you. I am going to die soon. I am willing to go. I sometimes die now, and when I do, things come before me. I see what I should do. One of these I ought not to do is the picture such as you ask. I do not want it between me and the Spirit Land. I should not have it made."

Further urging was not to be thought of. So far as known, there never was but one print made of him; a gala day group taken some years ago for the late Hon. A. J. Splawn. Both photograph and negative appear to have been lost.

Su-el-lil's statement: "I sometimes die now," must be regarded in the light of allegory. He had experienced periods of unconsciousness, a floating

53

away, as it were, to other realms, at which visions of the past and of the future passed before him, regarded as celestial guidance, sacred and inviolate.[27] He was a "medicine" man of the old Indian schooling, not to be confounded with much of the present day tribal "medicine."

Su-el-lil was of medium height and had a square, well-knit frame denoting strength, activity and great endurance in his younger days. His features were clean cut, typically Indian, and he had a slightly aquiline nose. He wore his hair long, in plaits, indicating his adherence to his native religion which was of the Dreamer faith, a philosophy that never has been understood by the Whites. He was a very primitive-minded Indian, and was regarded highly by the better class of tribesmen, as well as by the Whites. His prediction that he would "die soon" proved prophetic, for he lived scarce two "moons" afterwards. He passed into the final Sunset November 4, 1916, three days short of one year of his return from guiding us to the hitherto unidentified, historic *Wahk-shum* Spring.

In May, 1917, with William Charley, a second trip was made to *Wahk-shum*, going by way of the ancient *Ah-soom, or* "Eel" Trail over which Major Bolon rode to his death on September 21, 1855. This trail also was the route of retreat taken by Major Haller after his defeat by the Yakimas, October 5 and 6, 1855. Major Haller abandoned his howitzer at the foot of the steep "cut-back," just before the trail enters the timber line. Concealed by the victorious Indians, this gun,

LOCATING THE MURDER SITE

although often searched for, never has been found notwithstanding wild rumors to the contrary.

The day of starting was beautiful, and this time we had a pack horse. Crossing a wide slope of desert, the noon stop was on an extensive scrub oak flat bordering the foot of the Satus-Toppenish dividing ridge. Wild grass was abundant, and the horses were turned loose to fill up, while we lunched in the shade of the oaks.

Before us spread the upper reaches of the great reservation plain, extending to the Ahtanum Ridge to the north. To the left lay the foothills of the Cascades [Range], and to the right, in close proximity, rose "Old Man" *Chan-ish*[28] and his two wives. The "old" wife, with papoose on its *"skein*: "bearing up,"—Yakima appellation for "cradle board"—lies with her back to *Chan-ish*, at his right. The "new" wife, whose acquisition brought ruin and disaster to *Chan-ish* and his budding Indian civilization, lies facing him at his left. The "Old Man" himself lies supine. The group and its legend is a remarkable illustration of the dawn of man's reasoning on governmental problems, and the gradual evolving of community and social laws.

When we were ready to go, my horse was found standing with front feet on a splendid, almost new, plaited rawhide hackamore, minus a hitching rope only. As my equipment did not include a halter, this find by my horse was most welcome, and was interpreted as an augury of a safe and successful trip.

The "cut-back" of the Eel Trail was a stiff

climb, but worth the effort, as from the summit of the mountain was a magnificent view in all directions. Here a pause was made to "blow" the horses and to pay proper homage at the ancient invocatory shrine—a small heap of stones—beside the trail. We left offerings of good will to insure the success of our undertaking. From there to our destination no trouble was experienced in keeping to the ancient Indian thorough fare all the way, although many sections were overgrown and choked with young pines.

A small mountain meadow or prairie [was] crossed which was known to the Indians as *Ich-qee*, and also as *Kam-mi-hi-tash*.[29] It was a noted camas ground, and there they formerly congregated in June during the camas season. While the women dug roots, the men hunted and ran horses. No trace of the old race track was visible in the grass, but a seven-foot post, around which the racers circled to hit the home stretch, was still standing. It was here that Major Haller was overtaken by the pursuing Yakimas who he fought off for perhaps half a day. In that skirmish an Indian named *Ho-pee* was wounded in the wrist.

On the timberless ridge above *Wahk-shum* Spring, we found, as *Su-el-lil* had described, two small rockheaps, hardly three inches high; and the trail, now that the ground was bare. Several well-defined trail "traces" leading down to the tragedy site were in evidence. We camped near the spring that night, or more properly "springs," for there were a number of "wet weather springs." Which was the

LOCATING THE MURDER SITE

permanent *Wahk-shum* could not be determined. It was decided to return later in the summer to solve the problem.

The reservation spring horse roundup was closing, and from *Wahk-shum* William steered for *Meninock's* Spring, the location of one of the branding corrals high on the reservation tableland near timberline. We arrived at noon in time to participate in a grand feast which featured a scaffold-roasted steer and bitterroot, or *pe-ahke*, a plant that grew profusely there and was then ripe for harvesting. While the men rode in the roundup, the women dug great quantities of the root. After the feast, the Indians gathered for a council, and Chief Meninock, sitting a white horse, harangued them for an hour on the probability of the young men being drafted for service in the World War. Extension of the draft to include the Indians, he said, would be a violation of their treaty rights. The young men, however, waited not to be forced into uniform. Many of them volunteered, as did thousands of other Indians throughout the United States.

We returned to *Wahk-shum* Spring in August. Our route took us over Toppenish Mountain, across upper Dry Creek and past "Castle Rock," a magnificent pile overlooking Satus Canyon, and called by the Indians "Chipmunk's Burial Place." Isolated, it is seldom visited except by an occasional ranger or stockman. Composed of immense basaltic blocks, the Chipmunk is an elongated boulder resting on the apex of the main column and on a great boulder of nearly equal height. A planned scaling of the pile was foregone, when William said it was infested with rattlesnakes. The previous evening, when loping along a desert tableland trail in the gloaming, our mounts shied at an occasional startling *w-h-i-r-r-r* of these nocturnal reptiles, disturbed by the passing hoofbeats. A late ride was necessary in order to camp in the timber where danger from the crawling terrors was negligible.

Unfortunately, the legend of Chipmunk's Burial is only fragmentary. The story is that Chipmunk, a child (of the "Animal People"), died on the *n-Che-wana*: "big river," [the Columbia River]—and his grandmother carried him on her back looking for a suitable burial place. Not finding any to her liking, she placed the grandchild's body on the towering rocks, where it will always remain.[30]

It was understood that *Wahk-shum* Spring was on land of which George Garner, stockman of Centerville, Klickitat County, had charge; and it was arranged that he meet us there. Upon arrival just before noon on a Sunday, Mr. and Mrs. Garner and a few of their friends—and a splendid chicken dinner—awaited us.

The wet weather springs had vanished, and only the one that flowed continuously remained. This was *Wahk-shum*, of *Su-el-lil's* narrative, and we had no difficulty marking the place of Bolon's death.

All present agreed that the best location for the larger of the proposed memorial slabs—on which the

LOCATING THE MURDER SITE

circumstances of the fatal business could be inscribed—
was at the junction of the Cedar Valley and Yeackel
Roads, where the monument was erected the next year
by the Washington State Historical Society.

THE DEFINITION OF YAKIMA

Yakima, as contended by the tribe of that name,
was conferred on them by the Spokanes or Kalispells,
the last named being more widely known as Pend
d'Oreilles. This appellative is foreign to their own
language. The tribesmen—when induced to express
themselves—contend that any purported English rendition must necessarily be largely guesswork. But
after thirty years of close contacts with the best-
informed of them on the subject, the following would
seem the most logical analysis of the enigma.

Yakima is a perversion of *Yahah-ka-ma*; prolonged accent on the second syllable. The various
interpretations, such as "Blackbear,"
"Run-aways," " People-of-the-Gap," and "Succotash
Gardens," can be regarded as wholly chimerical. The
English rendition of the name in its original construc-
tion pertains to or denotes a "growing family," a
veritable "tribe expansion."

There were two geographical divisions of the
tribe. That [group], north of *Pah-qy-ti-koot*, (accent
first syllable)—mapped as Union Gap—were known
as *Pish-wana-pums* (accent second syllable), defined

TRAGEDY OF THE *WAHK-SHUM*

as follows:

Pish: "water worn rocks." *wana:* "river." *Pum*: "people." In verity: "people of the river rocks." Location, a "shoal" in the Yakima River, Kittitas County. "Shoal people"[31] as has been defined, is incorrect, according to the best informed Yakimas.

The bands occupying the valley south of the Gap were designated as *Mom-a-chets* or *Mam-a--chets*, a term bordering on the epithetical. The late Louis Mann, perhaps the best tribal historian of his day, pronounced its rendition as not unlike the English "coward." Mr. Mann added:

"When a boy I attended the Agency school under Father Wilbur, and we had our clan feuds. If a *River-rock* urchin sneered at a *Moma-chet* lad because of his clan affiliations, he had a fight on his hands. I do not know the origin of *Mom-a-chet.*"

V. THE DEATH OF GEN. GEO. A. CUSTER AND HIS COMMAND, AS TOLD BY OWL CHILD-EYEWITNESS

Sometime during 1911 a chilling account of the annihilation of a US cavalry detachment, and the shameful, coward's death of their commander was told to L.V. McWhorter by Owl Child, *Che-pos to-cos*.[32] A tough old Wishram warrior, he had lived, hunted, and warred with the Piegan Blackfeet Indians of Montana against the Sioux. But Owl Child's account very strongly resembles the final battle and death within a short time of Gen. George A. Custer and his troopers at the Little Big Horn. Shocking, unexpected—what Owl Child saw, how he remembered and then related the catastrophe which he witnessed may give extraordinary evidence how the Native American recalls his past—of the processes of oral traditional history.

....

"While with the Piegans, I sometimes went

61

with war parties to fight the Sioux.[33] I had joined the tribe and they gave me a name. It was *Che-pos-To-cos* (Owl Child). This name in Yakima is *Om-as-ish-tum*. The Piegans also called me *Shat-taw-wee* (a leader in battle).[34] *Shat-taw-wee* was a brave chief who had died. I was given his name. I was often in war. I will tell you a story.

"While with the Piegan Blackfeet, many war parties went against the Sioux with whom we were at war. I often joined with such parties. We would form in the Sweet Grass Mountains, or at Buffalo Head where we lived, and travel to the enemy country. There we would scatter, scouting to locate the Sioux. We watched for small hunting parties and camps. Finding them, if favorable to success, we attacked, killing as many as we could. Or, capturing a band of horses, we skipped for home. Riding fast we never stopped for long until out of pursuit danger. Seldom did we mix with a stronger party. A leader tried to avoid the loss of any of his warriors. That chief was greatest who returned to his village with scalps and horses, leaving none of his followers behind. No one liked the death wail in their own camp. Sometimes we were glad to return without spoils. I will tell you a story.

"We were a party of about seventeen under Chief Lone Pine, a brave and cautious warrior.[35] We had gone into a country a little strange to me. It was a large Sioux camp. We lay hidden on a ridge across from the smaller of two rivers. We were watching for

THE SUICIDE OF GENERAL CUSTER

stragglers from the Sioux village. We might get a scalp or two, or some horses. At the joining of the two streams or nearly so we saw a great battle fought.[36] Sioux and Cheyennes were at war with the whites. They had scouts out watching for soldiers. We saw these scouts come running their horses. We saw the Sioux hurry to where they waited for the soldiers. Eh! There it was—a dust cloud rolling in the distance. Troops were coming, but not yet in sight. The Sioux were on horses all ready. The dust cloud was drawing nearer. Yes, now came the soldiers! They must not have known how many of their enemies were in hiding. They came at a trot, the commander in front. They reached the flat-like ground between the two rivers. Not very large this ground. Eh! Eh! The bugle sounded. The attack came. Indians rushed from hiding places, the shooting began—loud yelling, loud whooping, guns going like bunched firecrackers. The bugle did not sound only twice, maybe three times. A bad mixup! The guns were soon almost a solid roar. Dust and smoke; smoke and dust. Horse falling; men tumbling.

"Soldiers were running, trying to escape. No use! Indians were all round, circling; warriors darted as hawks on flocked quail. No hiding anywhere. Blue coats; painted, naked Sioux, all mixing as waters of two rivers. Terrible fighting on both sides. Death everywhere. Not one soldier escaped. Horses were all killed. The commander was the last to go down. We had no watch, but where the sun stood, the battle must be measured nearly two hours. When night came, we left that place, returned home without scalps or horses. [McWhorter includes specific questions and Owl Child's answers at this place in the narrative]:

Q: — "You say the commander was last to fall? Yellow Wolf in the Nez Perce War tells me how, in one battle, he shot first the officer so there would be no one to 'drive' the soldiers.'" [See McWhorter's *Yellow Wolf: His Own Story.*]

A: — "We recognized him to be commander. The last man, he shot himself. Two shots to himself he made."

Q: — "Carbine or pistol?"

A: — "Six-shooter."

Q: — "Where did he place the gun?"

A: — "There was an argument. Some thought the first shot was here (indicating region of the heart), while others said here (placing a finger on his right temple). Myself, I thought he fired first to his breast. He raised on one knee, and then shot to his head. This time he did not get up; did not move."

Q: — "Did you afterwards cross over to the battlefield?"

A: — "It was a terrible battle we watched from our ridge—hiding. It was not for us to go there. When night came, we left that place; returned home without scalps or horses."

....

The historical narratives told by both *Su-el-lil*

THE SUICIDE OF GENERAL CUSTER

and Owl Child comprise oral traditional history, and reflect the Indians' points-of-view, their historical perspectives, and the selection of details about the past—meant to inform, not entertain. By oral traditional history we mean ". . . episodes of the past which the community remembers collectively. . . . [It] will be composed of a number of local traditions. These traditions may or may not be written in the formal histories, but their retention is chiefly by word of mouth, and so they will diverge from the printed accounts, if such exist. Much or most of history on record would never. . . survive without the crutch of print. . . . But folk history survives purely on its own merits, because some element of shock, surprise, heroics, humor, or terror has captured the folk mind."[37] By oral we mean that the historical narrative has been passed on by word of mouth over generations, across vast distances. Indeed, the Plateau Indian tribes possessed no written language. And by traditional we mean that this narrated history assumes a relatively fixed form as it circulates among members of a particular group. More, the narrated history must be authentic, must be related by a *bona fide* tribal member whose memory is keen enough, whose recollections are strong enough, that he/she remembers the old ways and lore of the tribe. But oral traditional history reveals a striking characteristic of a "sense of the seen," as from a *observer-participant*. Both *Su-el-lil* and Owl Child's accounts comprise oral traditional history because their contents are highly visual, con-

TRAGEDY OF THE *WAHK-SHUM*

crete details abound; a strong sense of place is evident; particulars from within the account reveal a great amount of authenticating detail; and acute powers of memory help preserve each account over considerable periods of time.

Oral traditional history accounts like those of *Su-el-lil* and Owl Child demonstrate extraordinary knowledge of and unique perspective on violent deeds over which darkness lingers in written history. First, a strong visual orientation focuses on observed particulars, on a spatial order of mayhem of a murder, or of a fierce battle. And, indeed, action marks both accounts. Second, an extraordinary recall of details attests to the power of memory by *Su-el-lil* and Owl Child. Third, the medium for these tribal annals is oral tradition. This is history which is narrated, performed rather, again and again before groups of listeners. And the oral traditional history episodes of both *Sul-el-lil* and of Owl Child assume a relatively fixed form within a narrative framework. Moreover, these oral traditional history episodes purport to describe real events in a straightforward manner which sharply contrasts with the style, setting, and characters as are found in "magic" folktales. Fourth, *Su-el-lil* and Owl Child's traditional annals provide previously unknown details of the murder of Bolon and the demise of Custer. But the historical validity of these two accounts requires: a) corroboration from historical records of the time; b) corroboration from archaeological field investigations. On the basis of his highly detailed

THE SUICIDE OF GENERAL CUSTER

description of the murder event, *Su-el-lil's* account was substantiated by means of his wintertime journey leading McWhorter and son-in-law William Charley to the murder site, and by his further descriptions of particular details marking that snow-covered site, which were subsequently verified in summer. *Su-el-lil's* oral traditional history account was accepted by the Washington State Historical Society, and marker stones were laid at official ceremonies. Likewise, according to initial historical and archaeological corroboration, considerable agreement exists between Owl Child's oral traditional history account and known history surrounding the Battle of the Little Big Horn.

Owl Child and his companions were eyewitnesses to a well-known account from recent written history. As with *Su-el-lil's*, Owl Child's traditional history narrative reveals a "sense of the seen," of the Indian *observer-participant* watching the annihilation by hordes of hostile Indian warriors of Gen. George A. Custer and his force at the Battle of the Little Bighorn, Montana Territory, 25-26 June 1876. And as with *Su-el-lil's*, Owl Child's narrative is oral, also traditional. First, Owl Child's narrated account is one of many which he narrated to McWhorter over a fifteen-year period. And not only oral traditional history, Owl Child was an able raconteur of magical tales, and more.[38] Second, if but one version of Owl Child's narrative survived, traditionality of account is also promised from other primary witnesses to the massacre: the seventeen Piegan Blackfeet warriors

TRAGEDY OF THE *WAHK-SHUM*

accompanying Owl Child. More tellingly, his narrative reveals a traditional shape, a framework.

But Owl Child's account cries out for corroboration according to internal details. First, important details of opposing leaders and their tribal identifications are lacking, factual details which would suit an historian's taste. But neither Custer nor his foes seem to have fully realized beforehand the identity of the other before Custer blundered into the hostile Indians' encampment. Within hardly more than an hour all was death and silence. Second, what makes Owl Child's account noteworthy—he was witness to details which have hitherto escaped historians—is the tenacious hold in memory of an incident he had witnessed 35 years earlier.[39] And upon reducing Owl Child's oral traditional history account to a broad outline, his observed details can be tested against other corroborative criteria. Great areas of <u>unanimity</u>; must be looked for, but also areas of <u>glaring contradiction</u>. (We believe his account is most plausible). An outline of the battle is useful here.[40]

    A. Details of EPISODE A   (Introductory Details) [Frame]
      1. description of the Piegans' methods of raiding
      2. description of one particular raiding party: leader, number in the party, etc.
      3. raiding party rides forth to area in Mon-

THE SUICIDE OF GENERAL CUSTER

        tana Territory not familiar to
        Owl Child
   4. other observed details:
        a large Sioux camp[41]
        location of camp: near
        intersection of two rivers[42]
        intent of raiding party

B. Details of EPISODE B: a battle of allied Sioux and Cheyenne Indians against a U.S. Army force
   1. observed details
      a. Indian scouts hurriedly ride in[43]
      b. Dust clouds in distance from "troop of soldiers"[44]
      c. troops coming forward at a trot[45]
      d. Indians prepare for the attack[46]
      e. the troop's commander noted at the front of the army formation[47]
      f. on a flat ground between the two rivers the Indians attack the troopers[48]
      g. a vicious, hard-fought battle—men and horses fall[49]
      h. escaping soldiers killed[50]
      i. troop's commander commits suicide: he shoots himself twice (a particularly observed detail)[51]

TRAGEDY OF THE *WAHK-SHUM*

    j. battle lasts only a short while[52]
2. the Piegan Blackfeet withdraw from the
    scene by night, ride away.

The validity, the reliability of both *Su-el-lil* and Owl Child's oral traditional history texts might be further verified by comparable traits found in the English and Scottish traditional ballad. The historical narratives by *Su-el-lll* and Owl Child both focus on a single episode, compressed and centralized, which recounts an account of sensational value.[53] First, they are taut in structure; economically, even sparsely stated, and the brevity of both accounts is striking.[54] Strangely to us now, neither Major Bolon nor Gen. Custer was named in the narratives. Yet, Bolon was recognized by the Yakimas he met on the trail. And Custer was notorious, hated by Indians—his distinctive dress and cruel ways were unlikely to escape notice—yet he was not recognized.

Both *Su-el-lil* and Owl Child's accounts are recounted in terms of action.[55] The leaders or the followers on each side in either account speak but little. But events come to mind, happen, follow one another violently, quickly. And with the finality of death and cessation of further action in both history accounts, each episode comes quickly to an end.

Both oral history episodes are related dramatically, but through action,[56] not dialogue. Indeed, in both accounts dramatic opposites occur. As the Yakimas travel the trail toward the riverside village of

THE SUICIDE OF GENERAL CUSTER

Wishram, Bolon overtakes them. He is recognized by some of the Yakimas, who plot his murder. First one, then another of the Yakimas attempts to dissuade the plotters. But *Mo-sheel* and others jump on Bolon, despite his pleas for his life, and slit his throat. His body is carried off and buried under brush, his horse shot. In Owl Child's account, the raiding party stealthily climbs a lookout point, and from there observes a huge Indian camp. Suddenly, Indian scouts ride in and much activity is seen. In the distance a dust cloud heralds the advance of horse cavalry. A battle ensues, and the soldiers are hopelessly outnumbered. Amidst the roar of rifle fire, the Indians ride after and kill fleeing troopers. Then, suddenly, the battlefield is quiet—the soldiers dead. At this Owl Child and his party ride off as quietly as possible in order to escape detection.

And Owl Child's account is complete in and of itself—there is no introductory segment, no in media res as if his account possibly derived from a larger narrative, and no extended conclusion.[57] Indeed, no preceding action or story gives rise to the action which is concluded in this history episode. Similarly, only as an aside is the anger of *Mo-sheel* recounted that Bolon had hanged "uncles" and "cousins" at Wallula [but *Mo-sheel* seemingly confused Bolon with Maj. Granville O. Haller, whose hangings of Indians occurred along the Boise River (Idaho) in 1854 and 1855.][58] And Owl Child states that the "war party" was looking to steal horses, perhaps lift a safe Sioux scalp. But at

71

the conclusion of the episodes (murder of Bolon/ annihilation of Custer's command) the Indians quietly depart.

Still another element of traditionality, as with the folk ballad, a strong sense of the visual is recounted by *Su-el-lil* and Owl Child.[59] Both were <u>eyewitnesses</u> to the historical episodes which they recount, and both episodes were related as <u>what-they-saw</u>. Their task, then, was to be as detailed, as accurate as memory would allow. Unwittingly, *Su-el-lil* was vouched for as witness to history past by Major Jay Lynch, Superintendent, the Yakima Reservation. [60] But instead of "truthful", Yakima George should have been described as *accurate*, his account of the Bolon murder exemplary of oral traditional history in which accounts of witnessed history are related as oral episodes subsequently within a tribal context.

Both *Su-el-lil* and Owl Child reveal an impersonal attitude to the events of the story, a sixth mark of traditionality.[61] Each episode is told, accurately, only for its own sake. But judgments by each teller about the action are absent—the story elements are allowed to speak for themselves. Indeed, the narrator may employ the First Person, but will quickly shift to the Third Person. But the facts, dramatically presented, speak for themselves—they are singularly objective. To begin with, Bolon is the first White ever seen by *Su-el-lil*, who does not understand English, not even Chinook jargon. Traveling with friends and family, or at least fellow tribespeople, he watches as

THE SUICIDE OF GENERAL CUSTER

Bolon is overpowered and killed. Remarkably, his account shows no emotion of just retribution at the murder by the Yakimas to avenge past injustices. Nor is there any sense of disapproval at the quick cruelty of Bolon's seizure and death, only a boy's fright—"I ran around, squealing." And he simply walks off at the close of the episode with his family—his overriding concern thereafter is to remain silent about the episode lest he be seized and punished by Whites for Bolon's murder. Similarly, Owl Child gazes upon a great battle in which Sioux warriors (and their allies) wipe out an entire detachment of blue-coated soldiers in very short order—in fact one of the great Indian victories during the Indian wars of our 19th century West. He narrates the action, the swift deadliness of the Indians' efforts—but no sense of pride is apparent at the Indians' revenge with the killings of the Whites, no sense of wrong at the slaughter of the Federal troops. Instead, Owl Child and his compatriots depart the scene, fearful of their own lives from these same Indians they had meant to scalp, to steal from.

Su-el-lil's eyewitness account is compelling for the details he provides of the murder of Andrew J. Bolon, thereby filling a void in the history of the region. Almost sixty years after the murder, in 1911 and again in 1915 *Su-el-lil* recalls of the murder which he had witnessed as a youth. Acute memory and detail persuade of the accounts' accuracy. First, particulars of a mid-September season and weather are recounted from fifty years previous: "It was about the close of huckleberry time." ". . . It rained hard all night. It was cold and chilly."[62] Second, particulars of the entourage, on its way to The Dalles [sic] (Wishram?) to get dried salmon, are cited: six men (by name), six women, and a boy (*Su-el-lil* himself) to care for the horses and to help his father hunt. Third, particulars of place are recalled: at mid-morning Bolon *overtakes* the Indian party at *We-twash-taw-us* [at or close to the present "Salmon Camp"]. As it was cold and raining hard, the party now traveled on together, ". . . down the trail on *Wahk-shum* Mountain [Simcoe Mountain] across a little stream running down the mountain, stopping [to make a fire]. . .at the spring below, at *Wahk-shum*. Fourth, particulars about Bolon given by *Su-el-lil* are numerous and specific: 1) he was White (the first white ever seen by the boy); 2) rode a gray horse; 3) was large, not fleshy; 4) had a reddish beard; 5) was a strong-looking man; 6) all the Indians shook hands with Bolon. Still more details: Bolon a) unbridled his horse to graze; b) fetched a lunch and came to the fire; c) left his saddlebags and six-shooter on his saddle; d) pulled off his overcoat and had on an undercoat (was wearing two coats?); e) divided and shared his lunch with the Indians.

  More particulars of *Su-el-lil's* traditional history detail how the murder was committed: 1) at Bolon's right stood Chief *Mo-sheel*; 2) at Bolon's left stood *Wah-pi-wah-pi-lah*; 3) *Wa-pi-wah-pi-lah* "tackled" Bolon, toppled him to the ground; 4) *So-quiekt* and *Mo-sheel* jumped on him, each catching an arm,

THE SUICIDE OF GENERAL CUSTER

Mo-sheel the right arm; 5) *Stah-kin* grabbed Bolon by the beard and pulled back on his head; 6) *So-quiekt* threw him a knife; 7) *Stah-kin* cut Bolon's throat. Further particulars relate of the disposition of Bolon's body, and the shooting of his horse; also of the division of Bolon's belongings among the four assailants. Finally, still more details relate of how the women had not stopped, had continued down the trail; of how *Su-el-lil's* father returned from hunting to discover what had happened, promptly left the group taking his son and his womenfolk—reported the murder upon arriving at Fall Bridge (now Wishram, Washington). To McWhorter was spoken *Su-ell-lil's* final assertion: "I can now go to the exact spot where he was killed."[63]

Su-el-lil's memory had been, seemingly, uniquely schooled: to observe details, to "read" or interpret them, to recall with accuracy. And *Su-el-lil* had a reputation for <u>veracity</u> and <u>dependability</u>. He himself explained, "I must have been about fourteen years old at that time, for I remember everything well." His peer, the Reverend Stwire G. Waters, a Klickitat full-blood, minister of the Methodist Episcopal Church, and chief of the Yakima Indian Confederation, told McWhorter: "[*Su-el-lil*] is a truthful man, and would not lie to you. If he said he was along, then he was there. I never talked to him about it." And of *Su-el-lil*, Major Jay Lynch, Superintendent of the Yakima Reservation for a score of years stated: "I have known Yakima George now for twenty-three years, and all though my incumbency as superintendent of the

75

TRAGEDY OF THE *WAHK-SHUM*

Yakima Agency, I [have] had dealings with him as a ward of the government, and can say with genuine candor that I always found him truthful and scrupulously honest in his every statement and business deals. I would not for a moment doubt his recital as an eyewitness to the Bolon tragedy as he gave it to you. You need have no hesitancy in making historical use of his story." ["Truthful" here = accuracy].[64] But second, not likely influenced by whites, *Su-el-lil's* facility with English was poor to nonexistent: "I understand but little English. . . ." Indeed, to converse with McWhorter an interpreter was needed. Third, not likely influenced by other Indians, *Su-el-lil* was frightened into silence about the Bolon murder. As he related to McWhorter: "all the long snows I kept secret that I saw the white man killed. William Charley, my son-in-law, was the only Indian I ever told it to. That is how you came to know and to ask me for the story. I was glad to give it to you a true history, yet, all the time I was afraid to talk. I might be hanged."

But the oral, traditional nature of *Su-el-lil's* account is apparent. First, the account was narrated to McWhorter through two interpreters, in 1911, and again in 1915. And both interpreters confirmed the "faithfulness" of the narrated material. Second, if the only oral traditional history version extant of the murder of Bolon is *Su-el-lil's*, other versions of the killing were most certainly in oral circulation:

A. PRIMARY ACCOUNTS: by *Su-el-lil*, also the five men who were present, or who participated in the murder.

B. SECONDARY ACCOUNTS: by the seven Indians not immediately present at the murder, but who were relatively close by—the six women (including *Ceates*, wife of *Mo-she-el*), *Su-el-lil's* father, *Wah-tah-kon*. Third, no record exists of *Sul-el-lil's* abilities as a raconteur. But his son-in-law was an able teller of folk narratives, and supplied numerous narratives to McWhorter.[65] But fourth, the very shape of *Sul-el-lil's* history account reflects its traditionality. The narrative is patterned as a framework, an oral narrative format frequently found in oral traditional history and oral traditional literature. The framework encloses the story proper and consists of preparatory details, and of concluding details:

I. INTRODUCTORY DETAILS, par-
      ticulars of
When / Where / Who

II. BOLON EPISODE
    Approach of Bolon
    Mo-sheel's response
    Stop, build a warming fire
    Debate on the killing (in Yakima tongue?)
    Murder of Bolon
    Disposition of Bolon's possessions

III. CONCLUDING DETAILS, particulars of Informant's
      father's withdrawal from party

TRAGEDY OF THE *WAHK-SHUM*

Assertion of *Su-el-lil*
Demise of Bolon's killers
Genealogy of *Mo-sheel*
Death of Informant's father

To prove whether his narrative was mere fancy or truth, *Su-el-lil* was taken up on his offer to lead McWhorter and William Charley, the old man's son-in-law and interpreter, to the Bolon murder site. Along the way *Su-el-lil* was challenged by numerous obstacles. (He could have begged off, but did not as he had given his word). First, it was mid-November in the mountains, the weather was cold, becoming colder; snow was falling—the worst time to travel. Second, poor health plagued *Su-el-lil*: he was 75, had trachoma. McWhorter was sporting a bad cold; William Charley was well, but worried. Third, foolhardily lacking tent, blankets, food for themselves and their horses, they set out on the morning of 8 November 1915. When their hoped-for night's lodging place was found to be locked, the three men were forced to spend one night in the open without bedding, without protection from bitter wind and freezing cold. But *Su-el-lil* led them to the place where Bolon had been murdered; undeterred by the passing of 56 years' time, by difficulty of vision, by snow and cold, or by underbrush which obscured the original trail now abandoned by the Indians. Unerringly, *Su-el-lil* led them to a small area which answered his specifications for an open-like park, with larger trees scattered about. Here lay the trail, now snow covered, on which the original Indian party had passed. Leaving the sheltering timber, *Su-el lil* led ". . . up the long exposed slope, over which the rising wind drove a downpour of swirling snow." And *Su-el-lil*, ". . . taking bearings from two prominent bald knobs, announced that he had made no mistake; that where he pointed out down in the park was where the white man died."[66] Later, when McWhorter and William Charley returned to the vicinity to search for the trail markers adjacent to the murder site during May and again in August, as *Su-el-lil* had described they discovered: a) two small rock heaps—the trail markers; b) the old Indian trail, evident now that the snow was gone; and c) *Wahk-shum* spring which, as *Su-el-lil* had said, was clearly evident.[67]

Oral traditional history accounts like those of Owl Child and of *Su-el-lil* demonstrate extraordinary knowledge of and unique perspective on violent deeds over which darkness lingers in written history. First, a strong visual orientation focuses on observed particulars, on a spatial order of mayhem, of a murder, or of a fierce battle. And action marks both accounts. Second, the extraordinary recall of details attests to the power of memory of *Su-el-lil* and of Owl Child. Third, the medium for tribal annals is oral tradition. This is history which is narrated, performed rather, again and again before groups of listeners. And the oral traditional history episodes of both *Su-el-lil* and Owl Child assume a relatively fixed form within a narrative

TRAGEDY OF THE *WAHK-SHUM*

framework. Moreover, these oral traditional history episodes describe <u>real</u> events in a <u>straightforward</u> manner which sharply contrasts with the style, setting, and characters found in the "magic" folktale, but which compares with many of the narrative particulars found in the traditional English Scottish ballad. Indeed, *Su-el-lil* and Owl Child's traditional annals provide previously unknown details of the murder of Bolon and the shameful, cowardly demise of Custer. But the historical validity of these two accounts demands corroboration from historical records of the time, and, more importantly, corroboration from archaeological field investigations. On the bases of his highly detailed description of the murder event, of his wintertime journey leading McWhorter and son-in-law William Charley to the murder site, and his further descriptions of particular details marking that snow covered site, subsequently verified, *Su-el-lil's* oral traditional history account was recognized by the Washington State Historical Society. Likewise, according to initial historical and archaeological corroboration, considerable agreement exists between Owl Child's oral traditional historical account and known history surrounding the Battle of the Little Big Horn, and Custer's demise—a suicide as witnessed by Owl Child.

NOTES

1. The hanging of *Qualchan* before his friends,
   wife, and father is recounted in Keyes, Eras
   mus D. 1884. *Fifty Years' Observation of Men
   and Events, Civil and Military.* New York: C.
   Scribner's Sons. See also Kip, Lawrence.
   1855. *The Indian Council in the Valley of the
   Walla Walla, 1855.* San Francisco: Whitton,
   Towne. Wright boasted: "*Quelchan* came to
   me at 9 o'clock this morning, at 9 1/4 he was
   hung"—there was no trial. The monstrousness
   of *Qualchan's* execution is reflected in "NW
   Tribes Honor "Quelchen" Indian Patriot
   Hanged by Col. Wright," 2, no. 6, July-August
   1970. The mythologizing process in the Ind
   ians' recountings of the grim incident has the
   hangman's rope <u>break three times</u> (the army
   record makes no mention of this). And not the
   rope but the evil power of a shaman did
   Qualchan in. DH

2. For a detailed account of Wright's death see Joel
   E. Ferris Sept. 2, 1956. "A Gallant Man, Gen.
   George Wright; Military Records,
   Letters And An Account of His Heroic Death—

TRAGEDY OF THE *WAHK-SHUM*

Picture This Stern Indian Fighter of the Region's Frontier Years," *Spokesman-Review*: 5-7. DH

3. Simcoe Mountains — Simcoe is a corruption of the Yakima word, *Sim-ku-ee*, meaning a low gap or saddle, applied by the Indians to a low place in a ridge, a short distance north of Fort Simcoe and visible from there. Their name for Simcoe Mountains was *Wahk-shum*, the same as the spring. Some of the Indians say that *Wahk-shum* is "only a name" and has no particular meaning. According to *Su-el-lil* and others it means the "head of canyons."

4. A manuscript copy of the narrative is filed with the Washington State Historical Society, Tacoma.

5. *Ka-mi-a-kun*—variously spelled: *Kamiakin, Kamiakan, Kamiaken, Kamiarken, Kamaiakan, Kamiahkan, Kamiahkin, Kamayakhen, Camaiockan*. Mrs. Sophia *Kamiakun Wakwak*, granddaughter of the chief, says that the interpretation is "Human Skeleton."

The Yakima Indians pronounce the name *Ka-mi-a-kun* with the "i" long and the accent on the second syllable. The last syllable sometimes is given the sound of *kan, ken* or *kin*. Many of the Colville Reservation Indians and those of the Paloos tribe, among whom the chief spent his last years, place the accent on the third syllable and say *Ka-mi-a-kin*, with the "i" short and accent on third syllable. His eldest son, the late *Tomio Kamiakun*, who lived on the Colville Reservation, said that the Yakima form of pronunciation is correct, as does Mrs. *Wakwak*, who was reared on the Colville Reservation.

Kamiakun's principal place of residence seems to have been on Ahtanum Creek, although he camped frequently and for long periods in Medicine Valley. A tree there was known to the Indians as *Kamiakun's* tree, because his lodge customarily was pitched under it. When a white man felled the tree some years ago, the Indians lamented its destruction.

6. *Skloom* (also *Sklum*, *Skiluom* and *Skoo*) held sway over all the watersheds of Toppenish and Satus (*Setass*) Creeks and over the plain extending eastward to the Yakima River and northward to the Ahtanum Ridge to the present Union Gap. His sphere of influence included the Goldendale district in Klickitat County. One tribesman describes him as "tall, homely and a great gambler."

TRAGEDY OF THE *WAHK-SHUM*

7. *Ow-hi* lived in the Wenas Valley.

8. Historians do not agree on the number of miners killed. Victor, Frances F. 1894. *The Early Indian Wars of Oregon*. Salem: F.C. Baker Co., p. 424, says: ". . .several citizens of the Puget Sound region traveling to the Colville mines. . . ."

   Bancroft, Hubert H 1890. *History of Washington, Idaho and Montana*, in *The Works of H. H. Bancroft*. San Francisco: History Co., Vol. 31, footnote on p. 111, says: "The first person known to be killed by the Yakimas was Henry Mattice of Olympia. One of the Eatons, the first settlers east of Tumwater was also killed, and other citizens of Puget Sound [too], to the number of about 20, among whom were Fanjoy, Walker and Jemison of Seattle."

   Professor Edmond S. Meany, 1909. *History of the State of Washington*. New York: The Macmillan Co., p. 179, says: "The first party, consisting of O.M. Eaton and Joseph Fanjoy disappeared. Months may have passed without such a disappearance exciting alarm if it had not been for the experience of the second party. This comprised L.O. Merilet, J.C. Avery, Eugene Barier, Charles Walker and a Mr. Jamieson. Near Simcoe, in the Yakima Valley,

THE SUICIDE OF GENERAL CUSTER

Walker and Jamieson were shot down by the Indians. The others, somewhat in the rear, hid themselves; and by traveling at night and hiding during the day, escaped, carrying the news of Indian hostility to Seattle."

Splawn, Andrew. J. 1917. *Ka-mi-akin, the Last Hero of the Yakimas*. Portland, OR, Kilham Stationery and Printing Co., p.41, says that the first attack on the miners was made by Qual-chan and five relatives, who "overtook six white men, almost at the ford on the Yakima River near the present dam of the Cascade Mill Company." Splawn states that all six were killed and identifies five as Jamieson, Walker, Cummings, Huffman and Fanjoy." Not long afterward two Indians "killed two white men on the hills north of the *Up-tanum*," and he believes that these two victims were Mattice and Eaton.

9. Snowden, Clinton A. 1909-11. *History of Washington: The Rise and Progress of an American State*. New York: Century Co., III: pp. 328-29.

10. *Mo-sheel*, also pronounced *Mo-shale*. The spelling *Me-cheil* has been used by historians. According to Splawn, *Ka-mi-akin...*, p. 65, he was known also as *Su-gintch*.

TRAGEDY OF THE *WAHK-SHUM*

11. The father of *Ka-mi-a-kun*, *Show-a-wai Ko-ti-a-ken* and *Skloom* was of the Paloos tribe. Their mother was a Yakima.

12. According to a letter in the Washington State Historical Society, Tacoma, WA, dated 8 October 1915, by Elizabeth Hall, the Smithsonian Institution, Washington, D.C., the correct spelling of Bolon's name is given: Andrew J. *Bolen*. Bolen had been appointed Yakima Indian Agent on 9 August 1854. A member of the first Washington Territorial Legislature from Clarke [sic.] County in 1854, Bolen had married a Vancouver girl in 1849, and had fathered two daughters. DH

13. *Wee-tal-e-kee*: "Moving-up," or "Leading-up," also the Yakima name for Dry Creek, a branch of the Satus which the trail follows.

14. *Yah-hoh*: "Marshy," or "Wet ground," [found] at the head of Dry Creek.

15. *Ah-soom*: "Eel."

16. *Thap-pahn-ish*: "Sloping-down." Applied to the land bordering the upper part of *Thap-pahn-ish* Creek, now corrupted into *Toppenish*. The *Ah-soom* (Eel) Trail crossed these slopes, and wound over the high, steep ridge which di-

vides the waters of Toppenish and Dry Creeks.

17. *Mool-mool*: "Bubbling Water," a spring on the site of Fort Simcoe.

18. *We-twash-tawus*: "Boiling-place-for-salmon," at, or close to, the present "Salmon Camp."

19. Up to this time there had been no hanging of Indians in the Yakima Country, but there was a transaction on the Boise river (Idaho), in 1854, and another in 1855, to which *Mo-sheel* may have been referring. His designation of the victims as "his uncles and cousins" would not imply, necessarily, actual relationship, as such terms commonly are used elastically by Indians and are applied to close friends as well as to blood relations.

The reference to Wallula is inaccurate. What *Mo-sheel* had in mind was probably the executions carried out by Major Granville O. Haller on an expedition against a band of Bannocks.

". . .Towards the fall of 1854 news was received of the massacre by Indians on the Boise River, of a party of emigrants. Major Haller, with a command of twenty-six soldiers, was dispatched to give protection to emigrant trains, and, if possible, punish the Indians. On the road they were reinforced by a party of mounted volunteers under Capt. Nathan Olney. They suffered many privations, but arrested a number of Indians who had been engaged in the murders. One was shot while attempting to escape and the others were hung on the massacre grounds, thirty miles east of the Hudson Bay Company's old Fort Boise. The gallows were constructed close to the pyramid of bones of their victims," Haller, Theodore N. 1900. *The Washington Historian*, [publ. by The Washington State Historical Society, Tacoma.] I,3:103.

In the spring and summer of 1855, Major Haller commanded a second expedition "to give protection to the immigrants and to search for other murderers." This time he pursued Bannocks as far as Fort Lemhi on the headwaters of the Missouri River, shot more Indians, and hanged others. In Haller, G.O. 1863. *Memoirs, A Brief Memoir of His Military Services, And a Few Observations*, Patterson, N.J., The Daily Guardian Office, Major Haller says that his measures of reprisal continued "until we had destroyed as many warriors as they had killed of the whites."

The emigrant party thus avenged was a small train led by Alexander Ward of Lexington, Missouri. It consisted of a score of homeseekers. Eighteen of them, including Ward and his family, were killed by the Bannocks near Middleton, Idaho, August 20, 1854. See Brosnan, C.J. 1935. *History of The State of Idaho.* New York, Charles Scribner's Sons: 120-21.

Haller had just returned from his second expedition when word of Bolon's death was conveyed to him.

20. Bolon, of course, had nothing to do with Haller's hanging bees, but his position of authority and his close association with the military easily could have led the primitive *Mo-sheel* to suspect a connection. Also, *Mo-sheel* doubtless looked upon Bolon as a spy, assumed that he had ventured into the Yakima Country to investigate the recent killings of the miners, and reasoned that, if permitted to return to The Dalles, he would submit a report that would result quickly in the launching of a force such as had scourged the Bannocks.

21. It always has been said, with what foundation unexplained, that Bolon's body, the body of his horse, and his saddle were thrown into the fire (the campfire) and burned.

89

TRAGEDY OF THE *WAHK-SHUM*

22. Many of the Yakimas maintain that the killing
would not have occured if *Wah-tah-kon* had
not gone to hunt deer; that he was the real
leader of the band and would have curbed *Mo-
sheel* and his adherents.

23. Nowhere in history is *Wah-tah-kon* credited
with reporting the crime. In his *Memoirs*
Major Haller relates: "The long absence of
Major Bolon from the Dalles caused me to
send an Indian spy into the Yakima District to
learn something about him. It was with difficulty he could get back. In the meantine an Old
Squaw escaped through their lines and brought
news of Bolon's assassination, and the collection of warriors from all the neighboring tribes
to wipe out the white people."

    Splawn, in *Ka-mi-akin.* . ., p. 44, says:
Nathan Olney, sub-Indian agent, " . . .sent a
Deschutes chief to *Ka-mi-akin* as a spy, who
soon returned with the much sought information."

    Bancroft, *History of Washington, Idaho,
and Montana*, XXXI: 110, says: "Nathan Olney
. . . sent out an indian spy, who returned with
the information that Bolon had been murdered
while returning to The Dalles, by order of
Kamiakin and by the hand of his nephew, a son

of *Ow-hi*, his half-brother, and a chief of the Umatillas, who shot him in the back while pretending to escort him on his homeward journey, cut his throat, killed his horse, and burned both bodies, together with whatever property was attached to either."

It is possible that the "Old Squaw" mentioned by Major Haller was one of the women accompanying *Wah-tah-kon*. He sent her across the river to the fort to report the murder rather than to go himself and risk seizure by the soldiers for his affiliation with the murder party.

24. It is claimed by some that these Indians were hanged at Fort Taylor, on the Snake River, along with other Indian prisoners. Major Jay Lynch, former superintendent, Yakima Indian Agency, stated (unofficially) to the writer that such was the case. But in the absence of an actual knowledge of facts, it is logical to infer that the executions took place at the local military post figuring in the capture, and also because of the supposed cowing effect that the exhibition would have on the disaffected tribesmen.

25. Chief *Yoom-tee-bee*: "Bitten-by-a-grizzly-bear", was a prominent Yakima chief, who died on

TRAGEDY OF THE *WAHK-SHUM*

March 10, 1910. His daughter, Cecilia *Totus*, a resident of the Yakima Reservation, is the only living descendant of *Mo-sheel*. At the time of *Yoom-tee-bee's* death, a half-brother of *Mo-sheel*, named *Yet-te-mo-chet*, was still living on the Colville Reservation, and a sister, *Ah-ka-cee*, was living in Montana. Their father was Chief *Show-a-wai Ko-ti-a-ken*. Several months after *Yoom-tee-bee* died, a relative, Homer Watson, was chosen to succeed him to the chieftainship. Chief Watson's Indian name is *Chi-misha*, "Sinew Bow."

Wan-tah, the Klikitat who betrayed *Mo-sheel* to the soldiers, and who was said to have fired the shot that fatally wounded *Mo-sheel*, in later years was stricken after having dinner with the widow of *Mo-sheel*. Before he died, *Wan-tah* accused the widow's son, young *Yoom-tee-bee*, of putting pounded glass in his food. *Wan-tah* was a noted medicine-man. His accusation, accepted as fact by members of his own family, was denied by *Yoom-tee-bee* and his kin, and never was proven.

In 1909 and early 1910, when the Yakimas were threatened with the loss of valuable water rights and a great part of their best irrigable land—threatened by rapacious White interests and federal legislation—it was Chief

92

Yoom-tee-bee who, with a handful of desperate Indians, decided to stage an uprising that would call nation-wide public attention to their people's plight. They meant to take the warpath, to do what damage they could to Whites and to White towns on the reservation, and then retreat to the mountains. There, they thought, they could hold out for six months before being overcome. Councils were held secretly, and much "medicine" was made in preparation for the outbreak; and then *Yoom-tee-bee* died, and plans for the rising were abandoned. See McWhorter, Lucullus V. 1913. *The Crime Against the Yakimas.* North Yakima, Republic Printers: pp. 8-29.

26. For an expose of white homesteading on Indian lands in Cedar Valley [near modern Goldendale, Washington], see McWhorter, *Crime. . .*, Note 7: 21-22.

27. For a collection of oral accounts of these visions see Hines, D.M. 1991. "Some Southern Plateau Tribal Tales Recounting the Death Journey Vision," *Northwest Anthropological Research Notes*, 25:31-56. A version of this article appears as "Some Mid-Columbia Tribal Tales Recounting the Death Journey Vision," in Hines, D.M. 1993. *Magic in the Mountains, The Yakima Shaman: Power &*

Practice (Issaquah, WA: Great Eagle Publishing Inc.: pp. 171-206. DH

28. *Chan-ish*: "Newly married. This peak is also known as *Shu-puh-ka-niex*: "laid down [supine] by someone else."

29. No interpretation was obtained for either of names given.

30. Given to McWhorter by William Charley, this legend, "Chipmunk's Burial Ground," appears in Hines, D.M. 1992. *Ghost Voices: Yakima Indian Myths, Legends, Humor, and Hunting Stories.* Issaquah: Great Eagle Publishing, Inc.: pp. 102-103. DH

31. ". . . Pishwana-pum in the Yakima language signifies "shoal people." The name refers to a shoal in the Yakima River near Ellensburg." *Fourteenth Annual Report of the Bureau of Ethnology*, 1892-93. Washington, D.C., part 2, p. 736.

32. Also known by his English name, Alec McCoy, in his autobiography Owl Child recalls: "I was born at the Dalles, Oregon; we call the place Wasco. I was born on the site of the old Wishom village which was burned by the soldiers during the Yakima War, 1855-56. My father, *Pul-Kus*, was of the Wishom tribe,

THE SUICIDE OF GENERAL CUSTER

while my mother, *An-nee-swolla* was a Wasco
woman." [All notes hereafter are by DH.]

33. See Ault, Nelson A. 1959. *The Papers of Lucullus
    Virgil McWhorter*. Pullman: Friends of the
    Library, State College of Washington. The
    excerpt beginning here, listed as 37/1534, and
    is dated July 13, 1911.

34. He won the title of "chief" by taking three guns
    from the Crees in battle on the Red River in
    Northern Montana. He also took guns while
    fighting the Crows on the Sun River, Montana.
    He had distinction as a warrior. He sometimes
    wore a Cree scalp at his temple.

35. "Was It Custer's Last Stand," *Papers*, 38/1534:
    July 13, 1911.

36. What follows appears to be an eyewitness
    account of the annihilation of the forces led by
    Gen. George A. Custer in the Battle of the
    Little Bighorn, Montana Territory, 25-26 June
    1876. At best this account is a true eyewitness
    account by Owl Child, particularly as he cites
    observed details of a large Sioux camp, specif-
    ic topography including the confluence of the
    two small rivers, the flat of the ground, and of
    the cavalry troop approaching, etc. At the
    least, if a borrowed narrative, the account

which Owl Child gives us may be no less valuable in that it remains an account related widely by Indians who took part in the battle. Of greatest interest is Owl Child's detailed description of Custer's suicide, seen from a distance.

37. Dorson, Richard M 1971. "Local History and Folklore," in *American Folklore and the Historian*. Chicago: University of Chicago Press, p. 150. And see also Hines, D.M. 1990. "Native American Narrratives of First Encounters with Whites," *Journal of the Folklore and History Section of the American Folklore Society*, 7:31-44.

38. For examples of narratives related by Owl Child to McWhorter see Hines, D.M. 1987. "Accounts of Heroes and of Great Deeds from the Yakima Indian Nation," *Fabula*, 28:293-306. And in Hines, D.M. 1991. *The Forgotten Tribes, Oral Tales of the Teninos and Adjacent Mid-Columbia River Indian Nations*. Issaquah: Great Eagle Publishing, Inc., see also tales 9, 10A,10B, 11A, 11B. (Especially texts 11A, 11B are striking examples of the Oedipus folktale told among Native Americans, but which, many centuries earlier and across the world, a version had been adapted by Sophocles into his tragedy of *Oedipus Rex*). And see

THE SUICIDE OF GENERAL CUSTER

also in our *Ghost Voices, Yakima Indian Myths, Legends, Humor, and Hunting Stories*, text 74, a hunting tale narrated by Owl Child.

39. Two recent works about the Custer massacre are useful here:

Connell, Evan S. 1985. *Son of the Morning Star; General Custer and the Battle of the Little Bighorn* (London: Pan Books, Ltd.. See especially Connell's extensive bibliography, pp. 425-437.

Jordan, Robert P. 1986. "Ghosts on the Little Bighorn; Custer and the Warriors of the Plains," *National Geographic*, 170, No. 6:787-813.

40. To contest or else to attest to the essential truth of Owl Child's account, his observed details are related to the historical particulars of the fateful battle. And see especially note 42 hereafter.

41. Connell 383: not counting the numerous brush shelters of young warriors, the count of Indian lodges exceeded 1,500 in number, but not even the Indians knew for sure. Estimates of fighting men begin at 2500 Indians and end with 20,000 braves. By contrast, Custer led 220 or 225 troopers—the count is indecisive as some troopers later died of their wounds, and other

troopers are missing.

Jordan, p. 792: the village(s) of the Sioux and their allies spread "... for perhaps three miles along the river. Its population is now estimated to have been more than 7,000, with as many as 2,000 warriors. ...."

42. Connell 401-402: two streams run through the area: Rosebud Creek, and the Little Bighorn River (whose course has changed since Custer's demise). Jordan 792: the Little Big Horn River and Rosebud Creek intersect near the southerly end of the Little Big Horn Valley. The two water courses are clearly shown on a sketch by the Indian warrior White Bird years after the battle, p. 795.

43. Connell 412-414: according to some Indians, the Indians had had Custer's force under observation for several days prior to the battle. This may have been quite easy thanks to the dust cloud which the cavalry troopers raised. See note 44 hereafter.

44. Connell 269-271: Custer's force exhibited great carelessness in their travel, for they advertized their presence with boxes of hardtack lost on the way, also "whistling, hallooing, frying pans banging against saddles during ...the night march. . .," braying animals, campfires

the morning of 25 June. See also p. 414: the warrior Gall cited the dust cloud raised by Custer's force.

45. Connell 275: Benteen's last view of Custer's battalion was of Lt. Algernon Smith and company riding off at a gallop. Also, p. 355: Custer, last seen, was ahorse. See also p. 405. Custer's forces had ridden in a column of fours or, in rougher terrain, in a column of twos.

46. Connell 413-416: the Indians possessed presentiments of an impending battle through dreams, but also likely had far better scouting reports of Custer, than Custer had of his foes. For example, see p. 7: while attempting to attack the southerly edge of the Indian encampment, Reno's troopers were met by hundreds of Sioux warriors plus their allies.

47. Connell 354: Indians who attacked at the Little Big Horn did not know who Custer was when he fell. Only afterwards did they discover who their foe had been. See also p. 372f. On page 414: the warrior chief Gall related that he had no idea who was leading the horse company. Custer was not recognized. On page 54: again, the Indians were aware that they had fought and defeated a bluecoat force, but did not realize that they had fought Custer. Jordan

797: the Indians were unaware until after the battle who their foe had been.

48. Connell 7/274: likely, this was the initial Indian counterattack against Major Marcus Reno over the flat ground adjacent to the Little Big Horn River at the south edge of the huge Indian encampment. Most other cavalrymen sought refuge on hilltops, in ravines, etc.

49. Connell 383: Custer's force died fighting a defensive battle(s). And on pp. 278-314 from his bibliography, Connell details direct observations of the battle scene. Troopers died running away, troopers died trying to hide, troopers died staying and fighting. Overwhelming numbers of Indians swarmed over the battlefield to the attack.

50. Connell 278-314. Jordan 796ff.: according to modern archaeological examinations of the battlesite, "the soldiers were relatively stationary, while the Indians moved freely about as they overran one position after another."

51. Connell 374f.: concerning Custer's last moment little is known. He had two wounds: in the side, in the head. And he reputedly lay, stripped of his clothing, with a smile on his face. On p. 308 Connell cites a number of

THE SUICIDE OF GENERAL CUSTER

Indian claims that Custer committed suicide. Still, on pp. 410-411 Connell cites particulars which contest Custer's suicide. And on pp. 389-390, years after the battle, self-confessed candidates for the killing of Custer appeared, including such as the *Unkpapa* Sioux warrior, Rain-in-the-Face, or the Cheyenne warrior, *Haw-tce-tan.* Jordan 797: atop Last Stand Hill was where Custer was found—shot twice: once through the temple, once through the left side. Again, p. 810: the killers of Custer remain in doubt although years later several warriors claimed the deed.

52. Connell 303: the demise of Custer and his troops was quick, within about an hour. Not having timepieces, but telling time from observing the height of the sun, the Indians related the duration of the battle with the distance ". . . it took the sun to travel the width of a lodge pole." Jordan, p. 792: the battle lasted perhaps one and a half hours.

53. The particulars of the English and Scottish traditional ballad here were suggested by Gerould, Gordon H. 1957. *The Ballad of Tradition.* New York: Oxford University Press. Epecially are we indebted to Gerould's wise observations of "Ballad Characteristics," pp. 84-130. See here particularly p. 86.

54. Gerould 87.

55. Gerould 101, 103.

56. Gerould 98, 100.

57. Gerould 87.

58. On *Mo-sheel's* inaccuracy about locale of any executions, see again McWhorter's note 19 above.

59. Gerould 90, 92, 112.

60. The Superintendent's remarks appear on page 20 above. But see also attestation to *Su-el-lil's* credibility by the Rev. [Chief] Waters, p. 20 above.

61. Gerould 116.

62. *Tragedy of the Wahk-shum. . .*[TW]: *Su-el-lill's* comments, as cited hereafter, appear on pages 25 ff. above.

63. TW: 30.

64. Two versions of account detailing the murder of Bolon were related by *Su-el-lill*: in 1911,

and again in 1915; the second version was deemed a "faithful" recounting after the first.

65. For examples of narratives related by William Charley, see our *Ghost Voices, Yakima Indian Myths, Legends, Humor, and Hunting Stories*, previously cited: texts 4, 18, 32, 33, 47.

66. TW: 27.

67. TW: 27

TRAGEDY OF THE *WAHK-SHUM*

ACKNOWLEDGEMENTS

A. I am grateful to Mr. John Guido, Head, Manuscripts, Archives and Special Collections, Holland Library, Washington State University, for permissions to publish the photograph of Owl Child and the manuscript portions of this volume.

B. I am grateful to the Smithsonian Institution, National Anthropological Archives, for permission to publish photographs of *Ow-hi* and of *Qual-chan*. The original miniature watercolor portraits are in the U.S. National Museum collection. Also, I am grateful to the Washington State Historical Society, Tacoma, for permission to publish photographs from their collections.

C. For their sharp-eyed proofreading I am grateful to Jacob Sterling and Alan Hines. All remaining errors are mine alone.

ORDER FORM

Great Eagle Publishing, Inc.
3020 Issaquah-Pine Lake Rd. S.E., Suite 481
Issaquah, Washington 98027
Fax (206) 391-7812

Please send:

_____ copies of **TRAGEDY OF THE WAHK-SHUM: THE DEATH OF ANDREW J. BOLON, AS TOLD BY SU-EL-LIL, EYEWITNESS; ALSO, THE SUICIDE OF GENERAL GEORGE A. CUSTER, AS TOLD BY OWL CHILD, EYE-WITNESS** at $10.95 per copy.

_____ copies of **MAGIC IN THE MOUNTAINS, THE YAKIMA SHAMAN: POWER & PRACTICE** at $17.95 per copy.

_____ copies of **GHOST VOICES, YAKIMA INDIAN MYTHS, LEGENDS, HUMOR AND HUNTING STORIES** at $23.95 per copy.

_____ copies of **THE FORGOTTEN TRIBES, ORAL TALES OF THE TENINOS AND ADJACENT MID-COLUMBIA RIVER INDIAN NATIONS** at $10.95 per copy.

I understand that I may return any book for a full refund--for any reason, no questions asked.

Name_____

Address_____

_____

City _____ State _____ ZIP _____

Phone (_____) _____

Sales Tax
Add 8.2% for books shipped
to Washington State addresses.

Shipping
Book rate: $1.75 for the first book
and $0.75 for each additional book
(Surface shipping may take three or four weeks)

Please photocopy this order form.

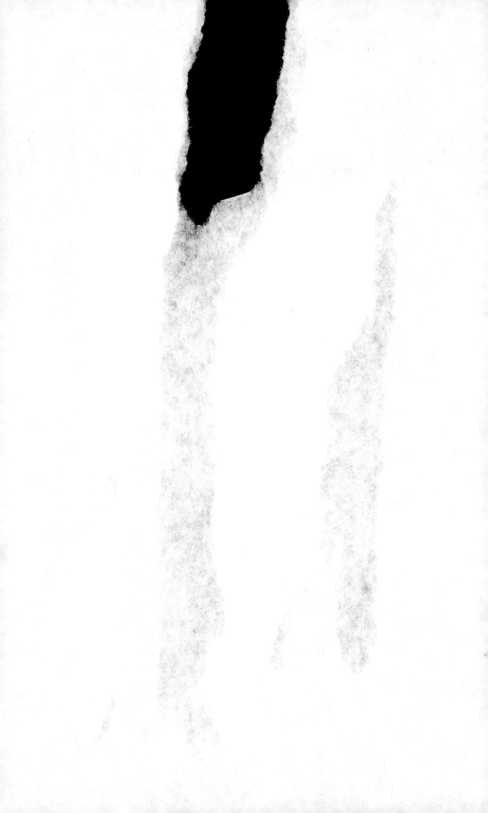